Xavier Barral i Altet

Series Editor: Henri Stierlin
Photographs: Claude Huber, Anne and Henri Stierlin

THE EARLY MIDDLE AGES

From Late Antiquity to A. D. 1000

TASCHEN

Köln Lisboa London New York Paris Tokyo

Page 3
Early medieval representation of
symbolic or real architecture.
Mural painting, San Julián de los
Prados, Oviedo, ninth century.

Page 5
The construction of the
Tabernacle, miniature from the
Psalterium Aureum, St. Gall,
c. 900. (Library of the abbey,
St. Gall, Cod. Sang. 22, p. 64)

© 1997 Benedikt Taschen Verlag GmbH
Hohenzollernring 53, D-50672 Köln

Editor-in-chief: Angelika Taschen, Cologne
Edited by Susanne Klinkhamels, Cologne
Co-edited by Caroline Keller, Cologne
Design and layout: Marion Hauff, Milan
English translation: Lory Frankel, New York

Printed in Germany
ISBN 3-8228-8261-5

Contents

INTRODUCTION

Historical Continuity

Aachen, the marvel of Carolingian Europe
Charlemagne's Palatine Chapel at Aachen, interior view, 790–805. The architectural vitality of the Carolingians, enhanced by extensive study of vaulting, receives full expression in this octagonal dome, which rests on a drum pierced with windows. The modern mosaics evoke the lost Carolingian decoration.

The concepts of Late Antiquity and the Early Middle Ages have undergone an evolution over the course of recent decades. The traditional idea that emerged from romantic historiography, which saw this period as one of discontinuity and darkness, has been replaced by one more congruent with current historical research on society. This view emphasizes historical continuity and sees in Late Antiquity an original civilization with its own character.

Late Antiquity is the logical point of departure for a study of Western medieval architecture, since this period gave birth to the Christian basilica. At the end of the first quarter of the fourth century, the basilica suddenly emerged in fully developed form as the place where Christians gathered and as a site for the veneration of the Eucharist, just as it would remain for the next six centuries. In the Middle Ages especially, the evolution of the basilica – of the church – was invariably based on the model developed during Late Antiquity.

In chronological terms, the present volume covers an extensive period, the longest of all the periods into which the Western Middle Ages is divided along stylistic or formal lines. More than six centuries, from the fourth to the ninth, represent the period that is traditionally taken to separate Antiquity from the Middle Ages and Roman art from pre-Romanesque and Romanesque art. We shall consider this period not as intermediary but as having a well-defined character and marked originality of its own; it transmitted the heritage of classical architecture to the main epochs of medieval architecture, the Romanesque and the Gothic.

There is, thus, a deliberate emphasis on the historical continuity from the late Roman world to the post-millenial Middle Ages. Art histories often arbitrarily distinguish between Antiquity and the Middle Ages, creating a symbolic split to which they cannot easily assign a date. For some, this split occurs at the end of the fourth or during the fifth, for others, in the seventh or eighth century. The period pejoratively referred to as the "Dark Ages", "the age of invasions", or "barbarian Europe" was a time of creativity and originality crucial to the history of Western art.

During the third century, the Mediterranean was blessed with a unity both real and symbolic, rooted in the person of the Emperor. The notion of a Mediterranean empire was often revived over the course of the Middle Ages, for example, in the Carolingian and in the Ottonian periods. By the end of the fourth century, this unity had been lost. The East and the West separated, and the Byzantine Empire lived a separate existence at least until the fall of Constantinople in 1453.

Notable transformations took place during Late Antiquity – economic, social, and, in the realm that concerns us, artistic. The period is the first stage in the movement from slavery to a feudal society. But should Late Antiquity be understood as the end of the ancient world or as the beginning of a millennium in which specifically medieval feudal structures appeared?

In the artistic realm, alongside the main creation of late Antiquity, the basilica, a new medieval iconography evolved. Study of the decoration of houses, of images from catacombs, reliefs on sarcophagi, and mosaics and mural paintings in churches

Map of invasions of the Roman Empire in the fourth and fifth centuries.

is an essential element in our understanding of the religious representations of the Middle Ages.

This was the economic, social and political context, when, in the early fifth century, at the height of Christianity's public expansion, the Germanic peoples swept down on the Roman Empire. They subsequently settled in highly Romanized territory. This period, between the fifth and the seventh centuries, has also acquired various appellations. In continuity with Late Antiquity, the empire was divided into new national realities that emerged from the organized union of old local elites and the Germanic newcomers. These geographic zones gave rise to the medieval division of Western Europe. And the fusion of Germanic and Roman cultures produced a highly original new culture.

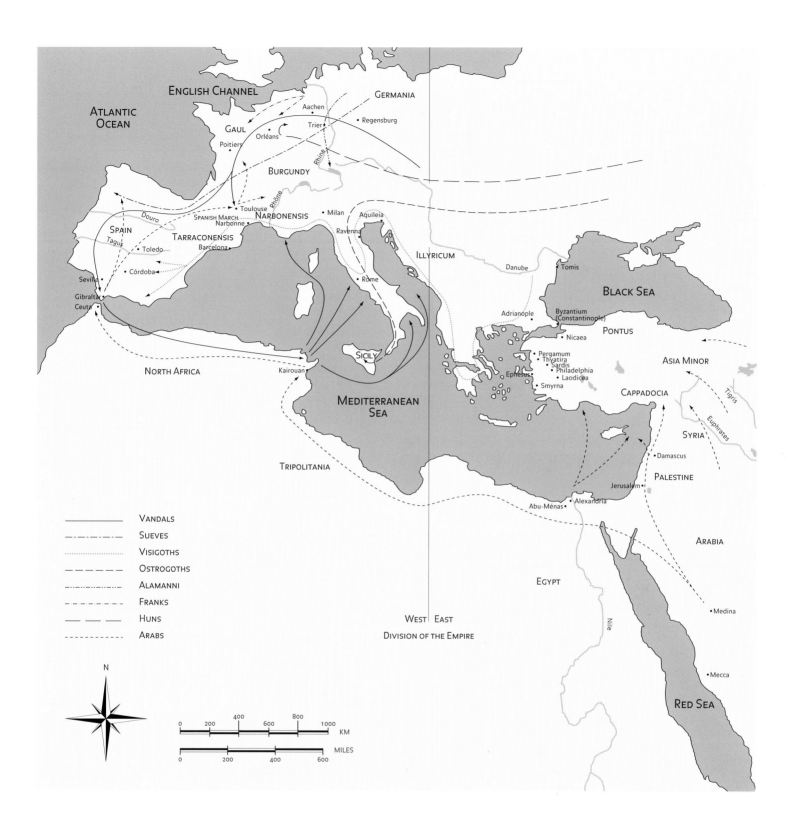

Map of Europe in the High Middle Ages (400–1000) with the main sites mentioned in the text.

Meanwhile Byzantium took on the imperial mantle and Constantine created a new capital, Constantinople. During the sixth century, under Justinian, Byzantium briefly held sway in Africa, Italy, and part of the Iberian Peninsula. Over the course of the Early Middle Ages, after Heraclius' Persian conquests and the iconoclastic crisis (disputes about religious images), the Byzantine Empire gradually receded from the Mediterranean. Like the West between the seventh and ninth centuries, Byzantine society sustained the memory of classical tradition until it attained its own medieval flowery.

In the West, the wave of Germanic or central European peoples divided up: the Ostrogoths settled in Italy, the Visigoths in Spain, and the Franks in Gaul. While the Iberian Peninsula, with the exception of certain northern regions, succumbed to the

Arab invasion, the Frankish kingdom gave rise to the Carolingian state. Charlemagne's forceful personality left its imprint on the period that took his name; certain forms of art, which developed in the highest circles of power, are also described as Carolingian. The dream of a unified Western empire resurfaced in the Carolingian period, and obtained the support of the Pope: it was later revived by the Ottonians. The palace, the aristocracy, the town, monasteries, liturgical reform, demographic changes, the centralization of power, and a strong cultural development characterize the reign of the Carolingians. It is easy to forget, however, that not all of Western Europe was Carolingian, even though most of the continent had commercial or military dealings with the Carolingian court.

Ordinarily, the history of peoples inhabiting the edges of the Carolingian Empire is treated only in relation to or in terms of the latter. Yet each region had its own government and artistic identity. The Bulgarian Empire, the Anglo-Saxons, the Danish and the Scandinavians in general, the Slavs of the north, the Moravian empire, and the state of Kiev, along with the kingdoms of the Iberian Peninsula, complete the picture of the western and eastern Europe that we call Carolingian, and which marks the dawning of a new feudal order.

Artistic studies on the Early Middle Ages center on the architectural evolution of the Christian basilica. Over the centuries, the basilica grew in size, as the development of the liturgy or the use made of the building by notabilities shifted from one architectural feature to another. The notion of the palatine basilica, a semiprivate basilica intended for the use of the ruler, gained significance at the beginning of the sixth century in competition with the paleo-Christian oratory and the votive or commemorative chapel. The most notable example is San Vitale in Ravenna, which inspired the Palatine Chapel of Aachen. The latter, which took its central plan and two-storey elevation from older models, played a crucial role in the development of Romanesque and Gothic.

The distinction between mother- or cathedral-church and secondary church returned its validity throughout the Middle Ages. By contrast, starting with such prestigious examples as Saint Peter's in Rome, the funerary or cemetery church increasingly delegated its functions to the parish church. Over the course of the Middle Ages, one of the factors affecting the architectural development of the conventual basilica and the monastery was the rules of the various monastic orders. The cloister, a descendant of the *atrium* of the paleo-Christian church and the porticoed courtyard of the Roman house, became the central organizational element of monastic buildings.

The cathedral was usually placed on the edges of cities, as in Rome. From Late Antiquity on, this rule also determined the location of the medieval cathedral and the disposition of the surrounding neighborhood. As the city grew beyond its

Representations of the imperial image
Left: Solidus of Constantine, right profile, wearing a diadem with soft headband and beaded oval cabochon.
Right: Solidus of Justinian, imperial bust, frontal view. (Musée d'Art et d'Histoire, Geneva)

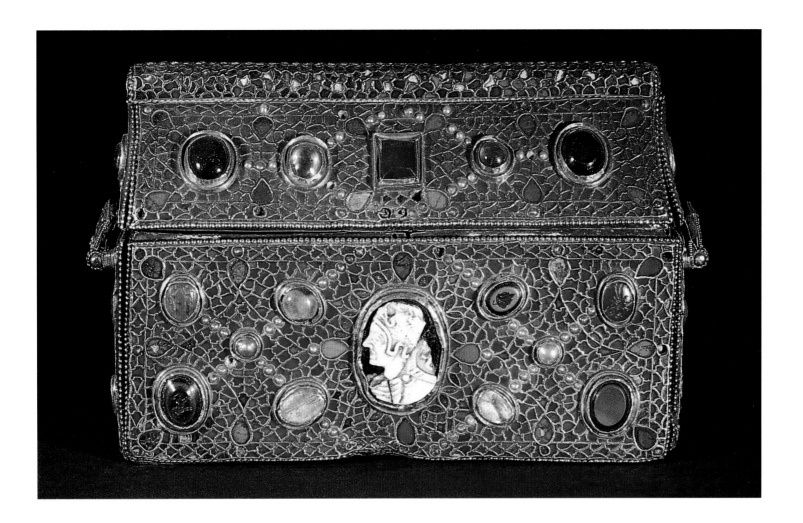

Cloisonné and glanwork
This casket belonged to the priest Teudericus. 12.6 cm high, it is made of gold, precious stones, pâte de verre, and enamel on wood. A large cameo is placed in its center. This is an excellent example of the technique of cloisonné, cabochons, and compound elements set in pâte de verre. Second half of the seventh century. (Trésor de l'Abbaye de Saint-Maurice d'Agaune, Valais)

defensive walls, it tended again to surround the mother-church, thus restoring the episcopal seat to the center of the town. Forms of course evolved, but the most emblematic constituent elements of medieval architecture were all derived from the paleo-Christian era. This period was regarded by the people of the Middle Ages as both a mirror and a dream of all that was marvellous; toward it they turned in perpetual regeneration. By constantly turning back to the past, the Carolingian period played an essential role in the transmission of that past. Rome remained the prestigious capital of Antiquity, but the centers of creation moved northward.

In art histories, the abundance of surviving religious architecture has tended to obscure the importance of other forms, civil and military, about which little is known. However, private buildings, urban architecture, and fortifications played a crucial role in the history of medieval architecture. Our view of the architecture of the Early Middle Ages is based on the small number of monuments that have survived. Under the Carolingians, for example, the effort devoted to civil architecture was considerable; that devoted to religious architecture prodigious. During the short period 768–855, roughly that of the reigns of Charlemagne and his son Louis the Pious, some thirty cathedrals, more than 400 monastic institutions, and about a hundred royal residences were constructed within the Carolingian Empire. Our understanding of the period thus derives from a tiny portion of this monumental achievement.

LATE ANTIQUITY

A Crucible of Activity

Page 13
Coins, evidence of style and fashion
Gold coin of Theodosius, with draped bust, in profile, a diadem headdress, and garment ornamented with a fibula. (Musée d'Art et d'Histoire, Geneva)

Roman Antiquity is traditionally divided into three main periods: the Republic, the High Empire, and the Low Empire. The term "Low Empire" has been – and often still is – used in a pejorative sense, in opposition to the brilliance of the "classical" period (the end of the Republic and the first two centuries of the Empire). The decadence that began at the time of the Severan dynasty, and which was said to have brought about the fall of the Western Empire in the late fifth century, constructed one of the major historiographical themes of the nineteenth and early twentieth centuries. Decadence and the end of paganism have often been contrasted with Christianity and the birth of a Christian empire. Nowadays, the accent has shifted to the transformations of the third century and the reorganization initiated by Diocletian. Thus, the term "Low Empire" has come to be used in a purely chronological sense, in opposition to the High Empire. The preferred contemporary usage, however, is the term "Late Antiquity", devised by Henri-Iréné Marrou to counter the notion of Roman decadence.

The notions of chaos, poverty, and dependence associated with Late Antiquity should be replaced by that of social transformation, and supplemented by detailed regional analyses. The economic relationships of the period are well known, thanks to the study of Roman ceramics, the export of marble, and the trade in amphorae. Archaeology has made it clear that the urban decline supposed to have occurred in the third, fourth and fifth centuries either never took place or was, at least, not on the scale alleged.

A city's fortifications can be interpreted in two different ways: either as evidence of the weakness of the empire's frontiers, requiring cities to protect themselves, or, on the contrary, as a sign of the wealth enjoyed by the city and its leading citizens. We should not completely discount the destruction caused by the invasions of the third century, but its scale has been exaggerated.

Thus it is essentially the increasing cultural unity of the Mediterranean countries that defines the period of Late Antiquity. Rich in change and reorganization, the period is characterized by symbiosis between its classical heritage and the new world of Christianity. Today, its culture and daily life are better known to historians than at any time in the recent past. Analysis of buildings shows how pervasive the Christian culture was among the local elites; church-building and the establishment of a Christian iconography resulted. Non-religious public buildings and administrative centers also continued to be built.

Decoration for the dead
Paleo-Christian wall painting in a catacomb in the Via Latina, Rome, mid-fourth century. Jesus and the woman of Samaria at the well of Sychar. This type of funerary decoration survives in great numbers in many subterranean cemeteries; here, we witness a confrontation between the revelation brought by Jesus and the Samaritan traditions.

The Historical Context

Late Antiquity begins with Diocletian's accession to power in 284. The period was marked by ideological confusion and the thoroughgoing reorganization of the empire as a consequence of the struggle to maintain the Roman borders and the unity of the empire. Diocletian set up a tetrarchy formed by two Augusti, or emperors (Diocletian and Maximian), and two caesars (Constantius I and Galerius). His main reform concerned the administration of the provinces, which he grouped into twelve dioceses. Municipal institutions and magistracies remained the same and proved recalcitrant to innovation, as the "Municipal Album" from Timgad for the reign of Julian (331–363) shows. Meanwhile, the army was floundering in the face of the numerous difficulties that it faced, above all the incessant attacks of the barbarians. During the reign of Diocletian, which ended in 305, and that of Constantine, from 307 to 337, structural reforms put an end to military anarchy and bureaucratic abuses. The court moved from one city to another (Trier, Milan, Constantinople, Ravenna). In 313, there was war between Licinius and Constantine. Constantine defeated his rival, and that same year conferred Christian unity on the empire by granting freedom of belief. From then on, ecclesiastical institutions reinforced their position at the heart of the community. Christian activity at the core of the empire was intense. Many churches were built, and episcopal sees, more numerous in the East than the West, were established in the large cities. Ecumenical councils such as those of Nicaea in 325 and Antioch in 341 were held in order to define new dogmatic and pastoral directions. Missionary activity got under way, and local ecclesiastical hierarchies, like the centralized administrative structures of the Church, were strengthened. The Christian church gradually became the meeting place for the community.

Finally, this expansion was accompanied by a resurgence of literature and the widespread diffusion of Christian writings, such as the theological research treatises of Novatian and Lactantius and the reflections of Saints Ambrose, Jerome, Augustine, and Hilary.

The Transformation of the Classical City

The society of Late Antiquity was not exclusively rural. It would be more accurate to describe it as primarily urban. In the country, large landowners owned vast farming estates, which carried the seeds of what later became the feudal system. These powerful landowners lived in the city, and over the course of this period the city expanded and grew rich. These cities that had suffered invasions in the third century quickly recovered. The wealth of local *curiae* (municipal senates) found expression in a surge of new building. At the same time, new urban monuments transformed the face of the cities.

Starting in the reign of Marcus Aurelius, invasions came one after another and civil wars between rulers were common. The countryside was devastated by poor harvests and other calamities. Despite this, the social structure held firm for the whole duration of the empire, and even after. The city, in the sense of a more or less developed urban center, depending on the surrounding region, was where the owners of the vast agricultural estates lived; this naturally led to frequent exchanges between town and country. Communication networks, urban lifestyles, and the agricultural techniques remained largely unchanged.

From the middle of the third century and throughout the fourth, new public monuments and churches were built in the cities. Many cities fortified their walls. The forum nevertheless retained its special status. Christian structures gradually · came to replace pagan temples. Places of worship associated with necropolises and cemeteries appeared, normally just outside the city walls, in the suburbs.

One of Rome's principal monuments, by virtue of its prestige and influence, was the basilica begun in 308 by Maxentius and completed by Constantine. Called *basilica nova* and set on a vast platform that dominated *the via sacra,* this basilica boasted three vaulted naves, the largest measuring 80 by 25 m and 35 m in height, and a fine elevation with engaged half columns. A semicircular apse at the west was designed to house and display the colossal statue of the emperor; the head of this statue, which has survived, measures 2.6 m in height. The magnitude of the volumes, the architectural quality, and the power of the vaulting made this monument famous. Light entered the building through the lateral bays – obtained by two rows

Roman imperial portrait from the end of the empire
Gold bust of Marcus Aurelius, second century. Emperor from 161 to 180, he intensified the centralization of the imperial administration. His reign was dominated by wars against the Parthians (161–166) and the Germans (168–175; 178–180). This kind of bust influenced the portrayal of men for centuries to come. (Musée Historique de Lausanne)

The Roman civic basilica, ancestor of the Christian basilica

The basilica of Maxentius and Constantine, Rome (306–312), showing the three arches at its northern approach. This edifice, barrel-vaulted in concrete and decorated with a coffered ceiling, enclosed a space of 4 000 m², supported on four intermediary columns.

The monumentality of imperial basilicas of the Late Roman Empire

Axonometric projection of the interior of the basilica, cross section, and plan of the basilica of Maxentius and Constantine, Rome, 306–312:

1 Large central nave, which reached a height of 39 m under three groin vaults
2 Aisles in concrete with octagonal coffers
3 Western apse, which contained the colossal statue of Constantine

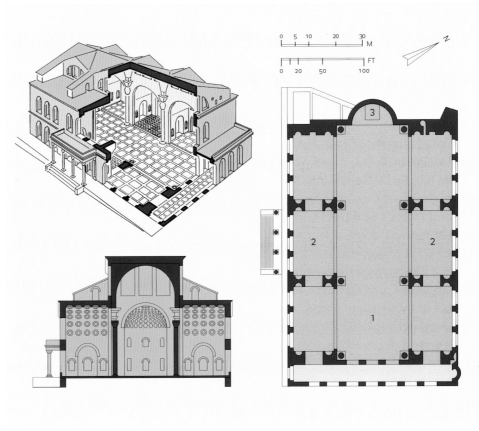

of windows crowned with semicircular arches – and from clerestory windows in the upper part of the nave. The conception seems to derive from the large *frigidarium* rooms in *thermae* (bath complexes) and its realization certainly influenced the design of the Christian basilica.

Besides the basilica, traces of other important buildings from the brief reign of Maxentius are still to be found in Rome. The emperor ordered the construction of a palace including *thermae,* a second basilica, an amphitheater and his own palace, located on the Via Appia. Other nearly contemporary buildings include the temple of Romulus from the early fourth century, on the Roman Forum, with a very original circular plan; the Arch of Constantine II from 356; and, also in Rome, the temple of Minerva.

Triumphal arches are among the major monuments of Late Antiquity. The Arch of Constantine in Rome, made of marble, was erected between the Palatine and Caelian hills by the Senate and the Roman people between 312 and 315 in honor of the *decennelia* of Constantine and his victory over Maxentius. This structure, 21 m high and with three arched openings flanked by freestanding columns, boasts an unusual form of decoration representing aspects of the imperial ideology. The upper part is ornamented with reliefs from a monument built in honor of Marcus Aurelius (the heads were reworked), framed by eight statues of Dacians, from the reign of Trajan, placed at the top of the columns. Medallions from the reigns of Hadrian and Constantine (the latter representing the sun and the moon, deified emperors, victories over the barbarians, and trophies) decorate the middle register of the arch, and personifications of river gods and goddesses embellish the side openings. To complete this description, we note that, as on the Arches of Septimius Severus and of Titus in Rome and of Trajan in Benevento, a large historic frieze runs above the side openings and around the ends of the monument. The irregularity of the composition and the stylized poses of the figures, along with the new way

Monumental structures for spectacles and circus games
The hippodrome or circus of Maxentius on the Via Appia, Rome. Its remains, like those of the Circus Maximus, also in Rome, illustrate the huge scale of circus architecture during Late Antiquity. It is known that amphitheaters and circuses were restored during the course of this period.

The victory of Emperor Constantine at the Milvian Bridge in 312
The Arch of Constantine, overall view, 312–315. This three-bay monument integrates a group of new sculptures with recycled older elements, showing a certain lack of unity that presages the advent of new styles.

The defeated, symbol of the Roman triumph
The Arch of Constantine, detail of statues on its upper part, 312–315. The low relief carving of the representations of episodes in the public life of Constantine foreshadows the sculpture of the Late Empire. The upper level presents eight re-used statues of Dacians, thus recalling the conquest of Dacia by the Roman emperor Trajan (98–117), which secured the Danube border.

CONSTANTINI MAGNI ARCÛS ROMANI RELIQUIÆ.

of representing traditional subjects (such as the speech to the citizens or the distribution of subsidies) point to the emergence of a new style.

Somewhat earlier, the arch of Galerius (no longer extant) stood in the new district of Thessalonica in Greece, and was built when Thessalonica became a capital under the tetrarchy. Of this monument, all that has survived is two elements of the columns, embellished with sculpted narrative scenes on four different levels. Also in Thessalonica, the mausoleum of Galerius (297–305) rivaled the best public architecture of its time in the West.

Under Diocletian, imperial architecture became increasingly conservative in the attempt to recapture the grand tradition of Roman construction. The majestic baths of Diocletian in Rome, directly inspired by those of Caracalla, are, perhaps, the finest example of this tendency. No less conservative is the plan of the palace constructed by the emperor in Split, on the eastern coast of the Adriatic, in or around A.D. 300. He retired there after his abdication in 305. Inspired by the traditional plan of the *castrum* and protected by a surrounding wall, the villa occupied a roughly rectangular area about 215 by 180 m. Square towers punctuated the perimeter wall, while octagonal towers marked the doors. The south elevation housed the imperial

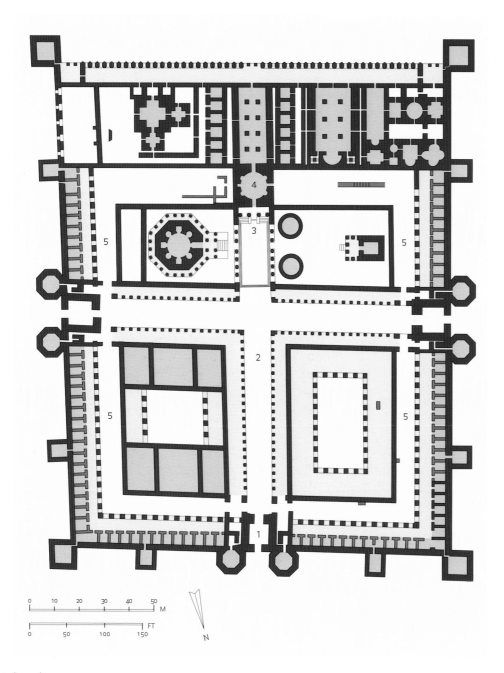

Fortified architectural complex in orthographic projection
The villa-palace in Split, Croatia, plan, c. 300. This vast palatial ensemble was built by the Emperor Diocletian (284–305). The formal entrance is marked by a broad avenue of columns, which encloses the courtyard preceding the vestibule. This arrangement gives some idea of the appearance of the entrances to the palaces of Rome and Constantinople of which nothing now remains.
1 Main entrance
2 Avenues lined with columns
3 Stairways leading to the pedimented portico of the vestibule
4 Rotunda of the mausoleum intended for the worship of the emperor after his deification
5 Courtyards surrounded by porticoes

Baths transformed into churches
Santa Maria degli Angeli, Rome, interior. The Baths of Diocletian have been converted into a church. It retained the groin-vaulted bays, the marble and granite columns, and the windows, as well as the polychrome marble veneer of the original.

residence and apartments; it looked out on the sea, to which the palace presented a vast wall with arcaded gallery.

Elements of military construction, notably in the section reserved for the imperial guard, and forms befitting a great imperial palace, are combined in this residence, which is on the scale of a city. Some features are reminiscent of the East, of places such as Antioch or Palmyra; others resemble the palace on the Palatine in Rome. It has been suggested that the palace's oriental air might be the work of builders brought in from Syria.

The architectural ideology of the palace at Split influenced other constructions of the same period as well as many later projects. The Christian basilica may itself have been inspired by Diocletian's palace, especially such as the area that runs the length of the central colonnade and, after crossing the vestibule of the residential area, forms a large peristyle. This space played an important role in the emperor's public appearances.

Other major Western cities also saw the construction of prestigious monuments. Among the capitals of the western empire, Trier, the ancient Augusta Treverorum, near the Rhenish *limes* (frontier) still possesses important buildings from the fourth century, notably the Porta Nigra and an imposing complex of baths begun under Constantine and completed about A.D. 370 under Valentinian I. The large secular basilica erected at the beginning of the fourth century is vital to our understanding of the architecture of the period. It consists of a vast rectangular room, extremely well conserved and restored, lit by two rows of windows, with a majestic apse that extends from the nave, introduced by an impressive triumphal arch. Outside, a portico or narthex completes the entrance. The structure gains its strength and rhythm from the flat, high buttresses, joined one to another by small blind arcades which

Emergence of a sumptuous military architecture
Porta Nigra, Trier, general view, end of the third century. With its large blocks of stone, projecting semicircular towers, and bays separated by engaged columns, this edifice is highly representative of military architecture at the end of the third century. With the addition of an apse, it was transformed into a church.

The basilica's unified interior space
Aula Palatina, Trier, interior view with restored ceiling dating from 310. The cement covering in use up to that point was replaced by a coffered ceiling, supported by beams in a timber roof with a span of 27 m.

enrich the outer walls. This monument was begun under the tetrarchy and continued by Constantine; we know that it was used by the emperor until 395, when the imperial capital was moved to Milan. It is essential to our understanding of the design and transformation of secular Roman basilicas and their influence on the genesis of the Christian basilica.

In the East, Constantinople, which was founded by Constantine in 330, prospered greatly during the second half of the fourth century and became the favored place for the new *fin de siècle* style. This style is apparent in the base of the obelisk erected by Theodosius I on the *spina* of the city's hippodrome in 390. The Greek and Latin inscription on the plinth reflects the state of the empire at the end of the fourth century. Scenes of the circus are found together with images of the erection of the obelisk, which was brought from Heliopolis. Above the plinth, the decoration of the base is organized in two registers, one above the other. *Augusti,* dignitaries, and soldiers occupy the upper level, while barbarians present offerings on the lower. The figures of Valentinian II of the West and Theodosius I of the East with his sons Arcadius and Honorius are shown receiving honors; their presence reflects the state of the empire at its juncture. The style of the sculptures here is continuous with the reliefs from the first quarter of the fourth century on the Arch of Constantine in Rome. In the matter of monumental constructions, the great palace and the alterations to the hippodrome competed with church-building; churches were very numerous in this city. Some of the latter, such as Santa Sophia or Saints Sergius and Bacchus were built as early as the sixth century, under Justinian. They were highly influential in both Eastern and Western religious architecture, though their impact on the West was indirect, passing through the western bridgehead of Byzantine art, Ravenna.

In the West, the Visigoths, led by Alaric, had been in Italy since 401 and occupied Rome in 410. The Colosseum nevertheless underwent a major restoration in the fifth century and Rome's paleo-Christian architecture and classical monuments have survived. The incursion of the Visigoths had little or no effect on its architectural habits. Not much later, under the Ostrogoth rule of Theodoric, new monuments were built throughout Italy. These include the churches, palace, baptistery, and mausoleum of Ravenna and the amphitheater at Pavia.

Page 23
Stepped domes in the Byzantine East
Santa Sophia, Constantinople, exterior view, 532–537. This basilica combined a basilican plan with a central dome, buttressed by half domes, each of which in turn rests on two exedrae in the form of a quarter circle. In addition to its imposing dimensions, it is this system of stepped volumes that makes Santa Sophia such an emblematic work.

Rural Architecture

In the Mediterranean countries, almost all property was in private hands. Throughout the period of Late Antiquity there were two types of estates in Gaul, the Iberian Peninsula, Africa, the Italian coast and in the East. One kind consisted of enormous agricultural estates, the other of small properties which served either as agricultural centers or secondary residences. Archaeology has revealed the remains of sumptuous villas, for example, Pedrosa de la Vega in Hispania, Loupian or Montmaurin in southern Gaul.

The most famous Roman villa of Late Antiquity, both for the extent and the quality of its buildings and for their rich decor, is that of Piazza Armerina, set in the hills of eastern Sicily. This patrician residence dates from the end of the first quarter of the fourth century. The scale of its conception and the refinement of its

The prestige of the honorific column
Base of the obelisk of Theodosius on the *spina* of the hippodrome of Constantinople, c. 390–393. The new style, first seen in the Arch of Constantine, is here used to represent barbarians and scenes from the circus. It quickly gained currency in privately commissioned figurative art.

The Constantinian style adapted to private buildings
Fortified residence, the home of the nobleman Junius in Carthage, fourth century. This mosaic illustrates the external appearance of a large private villa in North Africa, showing its façade with corner towers and porticoed balcony, behind which domed structures and other buildings are visible. (Musée National du Bardo, Tunis)

architectural forms bear witness to the vitality of private construction during Late Antiquity – and to the desire of rich landowners to imitate the imperial palaces. It was organized on three different axes; the buildings that housed the living and leisure rooms were reached by crossing a horseshoe-shaped colonnaded court. To the west rose a bath complex, and to the east, the residential wing. The latter, which was reached through a vestibule and peristyle, had many rooms, all of them decorated with fine mosaics. Banquets and receptions were held in another still more imposing wing.

The villa of Piazza Armerina can provide suitable illustration of the role that floor mosaics played in the interior decoration of these palace-residences. The themes depicted are the diversions and customs of the cultivated and privileged class, to which the owners of these establishments preeminently belonged. Scenes of hunting and fishing, representations of public games, Dionysian celebrations, and scenes of daily life are accompanied and set off by areas decorated with geometric and plant motifs. Other *villae* within the empire confirm the relation between a figurative and nonfigurative decoration and architectural function; in this respect we may cite the villas of Tellaro in Sicily, of Desenzano in northern Italy, and of Antioch.

On the Iberian Peninsula, many examples of large rural farming estates have been found. These include the villa of Fortunatus, near Fraga, work on which was begun in the second century but not completed until the fourth, or that of Los Quintanares from the early fourth century. At Pedrosa de la Vega, near Palencia, the floors are decorated with hunting scenes, at Tossa de Mar in Catalonia, there are similar scenes, in which the owner plays a prominent role. At Centcelles, a villa set in the open country near Tarragona, a private mausoleum has survived. The mosaics of the cupola, mingling Christian and non-Christian themes, give clear evidence of the Christianization of classical culture throughout the empire in the course of the fourth century.

The Christian Basilica

In order to worship in secret, the first Christians needed private sites in secluded places. Almost nothing is known of the sites used in the second and third centuries. The house-sanctuary of Dura-Europos and certain houses in Rome and Aquileia offer some evidence about the architecture and decor of such establishments. Not until the beginning of the fourth century do sources mention Christian halls of worship, which are sometimes referred to as basilicas. During this period, the term signified large meeting halls which were located in the forum of the city and used as courthouses and assembly rooms. Entered via a narthex, where the faithful gathered, the Christian basilica was timber-roofed and was divided into nave and aisles which were separated by colonnades; these led toward the apse, at whose threshold the ceremony took place. Large windows let into the walls of the aisles filled the interior with light. The axial layout and large apse were distinguishing features of these monuments.

Constantine's new policy in favor of Christianity, following the Edict of Milan in 313, encouraged the construction of major basilicas in the Holy Land and in Rome. On sites that bore reminders of Christian martyrs rose basilicas that functioned as *martyria.* One of the most famous was that built around A.D. 320 on the site that commemorated the Christian martyrs Peter and Marcellinus, on the Via Labicana. The plan of this structure recalls that of a Roman circus. The main building, about 60 m long and almost 30 m wide, was preceded by a narthex or portico intended to shelter the catechumens and unbaptized, who could not enter the consecrated space. The interior was divided into a nave and two side-aisles with apse and ambulatory.

In imitation of the models of the Holy Sepulchre in Jerusalem and other Roman constructions of the reign of Constantine, such as the basilicas of San Sebastiano and Sant'Agnese, the basilica of Marcellino e Pietro adjoined a large mausoleum of circular plan more than 20 m in diameter and featuring niches and windows in the lower section and *loculi* in the upper. The structure, crowned with a dome, may have been built as a tomb for Constantine before the founding of Constantinople in 325; in fact, it became the burial-place of his mother, Helena. Its plan and elevation are characteristic of Roman mausoleums – for example, the mausoleum of Constantina, now the church of Santa Costanza, in Rome.

The Constantinian basilica of Saint Peter is an even greater symbol of the early

Christian church than San Giovanni in Laterano. It was built to honor the tomb of the martyred apostle Peter, which was located in a necropolis at the foot of the Vatican hill, on the site of the amphitheater of Caligula. The structure is known through drawings and surveys made before its demolition during the Renaissance. Its construction dates to the years 320–340, after Constantine had leveled the area. This was undoubtedly one of the largest structures of the Christian world. It was designed to house the mausoleums and other venerated points of the cemetery that was located on that site.

It was a large suburban basilica with a magnificent *atrium* of four porticoes whose western arm served as a narthex. A long nave flanked by two aisles on either side was divided by four colonnades of twenty-two columns each; it exhibited a majestic transept and a large apse at the end of the nave. The side chapels were housed in niches that had been carved into the thickness of the walls. The scale and simplicity of its outline gave the elevation great majesty. Outside, a stepped roof allowed the nave to dominate the whole. Inside, an architrave crowned the colonnades of the nave, while those that separated the side-aisles were arcaded. The transverse nave, or transept, reached a height equal to that of the nave, forming a T-shaped cross.

Luxurious living arrangements in private palaces
Villa del Casale in Piazza Armerina, Sicily, plan, end of the first quarter of the fourth century:
1 Peristyle entrance
2 Polygonal *atrium*
3 Vestibule of the baths
4 *Frigidarium*
5 *Piscina*
6 *Tepidarium* and *caldarium*
7 Vestibule of the peristyle
8 Large peristyle with fountain
9 Covered walk of the Great Hunt
10 Basilican *coenatio* with apse
11 Small *coenatio* with exedra
12 Oval portico
13 Triconch *aula*

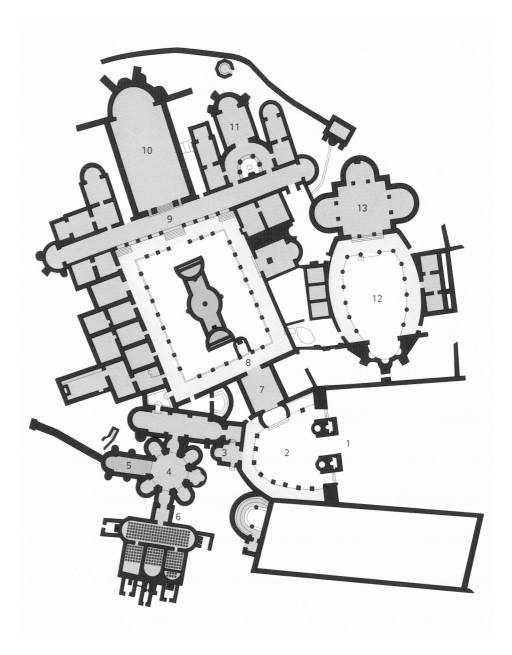

With the Roman basilicas of the Saviour and San Paolo and the great churches of Palestine, Jerusalem, and Nazareth, old Saint Peter's was one of the finest example of the new Christian architecture and exercised considerable influence in the Middle Ages.

The walls and the floors of the Christian basilica were soon to be put to didactic use in the form of murals and mosaics. The triumphal arches and the apses of churches could offer surfaces well suited to large scenes of synthetic kind which the assembled faithful could contemplate during ceremonies. Among the earliest known decorative ensembles are the mural decorations found in the basilicas of old Saint Peter's and San Giovanni in Laterano. The floor-mosaics of both the Theodosian and post-Theodosian basilicas of Aquileia can be dated with quite considerable certainty to between 308 and 319; in their architectural framework of a basilica with nave and two aisles, they deploy a geometric and figural repertory similar to that which also embellished the floors of private houses and tombs. The scenes of fishing at sea and the story of Jonah display an interpenetration of Christian and non-Christian themes which can be said to be typical of the first half of the fourth century.

The murals of the earliest churches in Aquileia have not survived, but the fifth-century Roman wall mosaics from the central nave and the triumphal arch of Santa Maria Maggiore can be taken as illustrations of this type of decoration. The wall of the nave is covered with a frieze of small narrative paintings in mosaic, thus offering viewers a continuous sequence of Christological episodes. The triumphal arch, by contrast, introduces the synthetic themes of the apse in more general fashion. The artistic development of large-scale theophanic images can be seen in other Roman buildings, such as the churches of Santa Pudenziana or Santi Cosma e Damiano. It is, moreover, also to be detected in the later decorations of Ravenna's important churches.

A model of a universal plan
Reconstructed general plan of old Saint Peter's, Rome. Preceded by an *atrium,* the Constantinian basilica was divided into a nave and four aisles by four similar colonnades, with a central nave twice as large as the aisles. A monumental transept with projecting arms preceded the large apse. The impressive proportions of this edifice earned considerable prestige during the Middle Ages.
1 *Atrium* bordered by four porticoes
2 Basin surmounted by a *ciborium*
3 Portico-narthex
4 Basilica with nave and four aisles
5 Small chapel
6 Transept
7 Apse

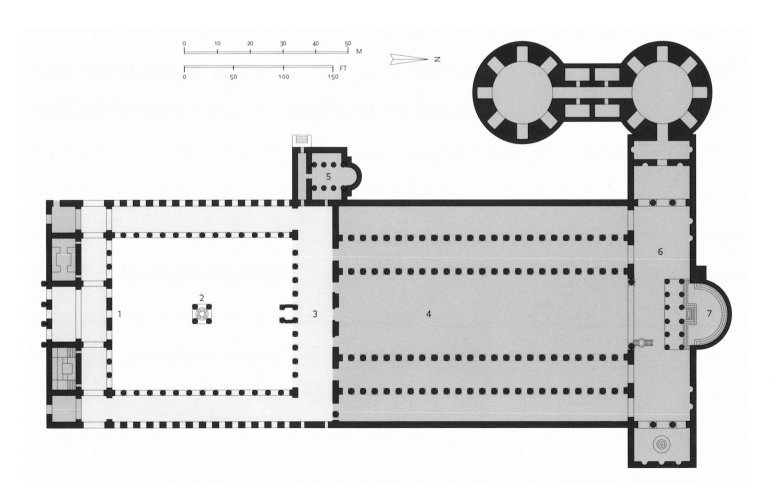

A completely realized model of the Christian basilica

The paleo-Christian basilica of Saint Peter's in Rome before its destruction, from a fresco by Domenico Tasselli, seventeenth century. Cross section of Saint Peter's on the Vatican showing a central nave, flanked by two colonnades with entablature and by double aisles separated by arcaded colonnades and covered by a timber roof. High windows lit the nave, but the proportions of the upper parts of the edifice are not accurately depicted. (Sacristy of Saint Peter's, Rome)

**Meeting the liturgical
requirements of baptism**
The Orthodox Baptistery,
Ravenna, exterior, first quarter of
the fifth century. The austere
appearance of this octagonal
building is enlivened only by
pilasters and blind arcades.
Its very compact volume was
originally much taller, as the
original floor is more than 3 m
below the present surface.

Page 31
**The decoration
of baptismal monuments**
The Baptistery of the Arians,
Ravenna, interior view of the
dome, third quarter of the fifth
century. Mosaic representing the
baptism of Christ, surrounded by
saints and the empty throne,
referring to the Second Coming of
Christ for the Last Judgment. The
dove of the Holy Spirit appears
with John the Baptist and the
personification of the Jordan
River.

The Baptisteries

Every episcopal seat or cathedral had a baptistery, generally situated beside the
main basilica or, in the case of episcopal groups, between two churches. Baptisteries were sometimes located in rural areas far from episcopal seats. In that case,
they were intended to accommodate the baptismal liturgy performed by the visiting bishop. The baptistery customarily belonged to a more complex architectural
group, whose parts fulfilled precise functions in the general organization of the
ceremonies. One entrance was thus reserved for the catechumens or non-baptized,
while a different entrance allowed baptized Christians to enter the baptistery of the
basilica in procession, clothed in white and singing psalms.

Baptisteries are highly characteristic of monumental Christian architecture, and
are not to be found in any other tradition. They are often circular in plan, and they
were the place of choice for the celebration of the rite of baptism. The baptismal

font occupied the central position, that is the position occupied by the tomb in circular or polygonal funerary structures such as *martyria* or mausoleums. A similar central plan was also, though less frequently, found in places of Christian worship. Surviving examples are the church of San Lorenzo in Milan or the Constantinian rotunda of Antioch.

Ravenna has two particularly interesting examples of fifth-century baptisteries. The older, the baptistery of the cathedral, also called the Orthodox baptistery, must be several years later than the middle of the fifth century. The second, the Arian baptistery, belonged to the cathedral of Santo Spirito, built under Theodoric in the last years of the fifth century or during the first decades of the sixth. These two surviving examples bear witness to the permanence of architectural forms associated with precise religious functions. The plan of the two baptisteries in Ravenna is classical for this type of structure. Here it is octagonal not circular, and is enriched by the rhythm created by semicircular niches, which give the impression of a square plan with rounded corners. The baptismal font is placed in the center, surrounded by an octagonal ambulatory. Above the central part of the building rises a windowed structure crowned with a cupola. In the baptistery of the Arian cathedral, a true eastern apse gives the structure an axial feeling despite the central plan, which is additionally emphasized on the exterior by an annular portico. No less important than the architecture of the Ravenna baptisteries is their decoration, notably the mosaics of the cupolas, both of which present the baptism of Christ.

The Christian use of Roman catacombs
Paleo-Christian painting in the cemetery of Commodilla, Rome, mid-fourth century. This scene of Moses striking the rock, one of many other biblical scenes, reveals the progressive Christianization of the iconography.

The Christianization of
iconographic themes and customs
Paleo-Christian painting from
the cemetery of Saints Peter
and Marcellinus, Rome, end of
the third century. The banquet
or funerary supper is one of the
themes frequently pictured
and one of the rites that the
Church adopted and sought to
Christianize. This painting covered
the tomb.

Funerary Architecture

The slow process of Christianization during the imperial period remains little known, and it is not until the third and fourth centuries that a clearly Christian iconography emerges. Study of sarcophagi and catacombs allows us to reconstruct the iconography from the early fourth century on.

At first, Christians chose images such as the shepherd or orant (a figure with arms raised in prayer) and bucolic themes, which could easily be adapted to the new religion while offering nothing to offend non-Christians. The Christianization of iconography occurred gradually and without displacing the old images. (The same could be said for the new architecture.) The sarcophagi acquaint us with the new iconography as, over time, representations of pastoral or decorative scenes give way to scenes of the Old and New Testaments, often arranged in typological opposition.

Over the course of the fifth and sixth centuries, Christian iconography attains to triumphal and synthetic images of divine Majesty; these are often found in the monumental decor of church apses. Among the earliest paleo-Christian cycles were episodes from the Old Testament, such as Adam and Eve, Jonah, Daniel, and scenes from the life of Christ, such as the miracles, concluding with the beginning of the Passion.

During the Roman era, cemeteries were placed just outside the city gates, as burial inside the city walls was forbidden. The catacombs were subterranean cemeteries built in the volcanic tufa of Rome's substratum. Such constructions were necessitated by the capital's lack of space and the expansion of its population.

No catacomb goes back further than the first half of the second century A.D.

The traditional arrangements of the world of the dead
Roman sarcophagus, third century. Christian scenes pictured on such sarcophagi announce the progressive spread of Christianity, which adopted the mythology and widely accepted models of Hellenism or classical Rome in both representations and inscriptions. Mentions of eternal rest and moral values facilitated this transition. The typology remained, as here, that of non-Christian sarcophagi. (Museo del Alcázar Nuevo, Córdoba)

Before the practice of catacomb burial began, the Christians interred their dead in mixed necropolises of raised tombs, as demonstrated by the tombs of Peter and Paul. In order to excavate a catacomb or subterranean cemetery, one had to obtain a surface property and be sure that the subsoil would permit the excavation of galleries. The underground corridors were initially narrow and confined in extent. They subsequently grew into a complicated labyrinth of corridors on several levels.

The catacombs are genuine works of subterranean architecture. Construction began with an access stairway, which led from the surface to the main gallery. When the intersection of galleries grew labyrinthine, new stairways were built in order to reach certain martyrs' tombs more quickly. These long corridors contained burial niches, or *loculi*. Small funerary chambers, called *cubicula,* were dug out for the tombs of a family or for members of the same social group.

Study of the Roman catacombs has increasingly been perceived as a separate science, a special chapter in the study of Christian archaeology. The chronology of a catacomb is normally the reverse of that uncovered by excavation; the construction of the cemetery was usually begun with a relatively superficial gallery, while the later galleries are deeper down. Supporting structures sometimes had to be built to avoid collapse and preserve the precarious balance of these multi-storey subterranean cemeteries. Moreover, the *cubicula* display imitations of the private architecture of contemporary houses, with false columns supporting false arches or domes carved from the tufa.

Starting in the third century, when the number of Christians had greatly increased, these catacombs underwent a period of spectacular growth. The old galleries were enlarged with secondary corridors, and *hypogea* and new stairways proliferated. Cemeteries were divided into sectors and in the late third century the dead inhabited veritable underground cities. Martyrs were considered desirable neighbours in death, and attracted many new burials. All manner of solutions came into play in order to gain space: lowering the floor of the gallery or surrounding area; raising the ceiling; or hollowing out the walls around a venerated tomb.

Light in the cemeteries came primarily from individual oil lamps placed in the niches or on small brackets set at regular intervals. But architects also created air shafts in the galleries or intersections, even in certain *cubicula,* intended to bring in not only air but light.

The names of the Roman catacombs offer an insight into the origin of the cemeteries as well as the legal title of their founders. In Rome, the names were of several kinds. A first group was named after individuals; these were perhaps founders, but with the exception of Priscilla and Domitilla, whose identity is documented by inscriptions, we know nothing about them. The second group comprises

Page 35 above
Mausoleum-rotunda from the age of Constantine
Mausoleum of Santa Costanza, Rome, exterior view of façade, beginning of the second quarter of the fourth century. A vestibule endowed with two side niches allows access to the ambulatory and to the rotunda, which is crowned by a dome resting on a circular drum pierced with windows.

Page 35 below
A plan like that of baptisteries
Mausoleum of Santa Costanza, Rome, plan and longitudinal section, beginning of the second quarter of the fourth century. It shows a circular dome with a colonnade that separates the central space from an annular aisle punctuated with niches and covered with a barrel vault.
1 Vestibule with rounded ends
2 Annular aisle
3 Central room crowned with a dome

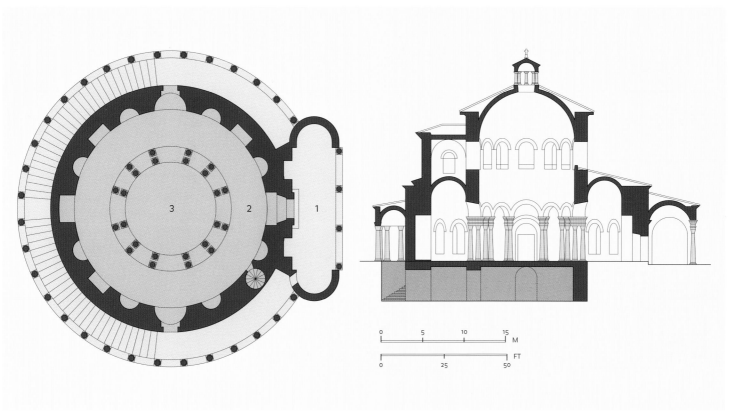

A work of art probably commissioned by a high-ranking patron

Mausoleum of Santa Costanza, Rome, interior view of façade, beginning of the second quarter of the fourth century. The vault of the annular corridor is covered with a mosaic, whose themes of interlaced vines, birds amid branches, flowers, fruits, and various objects stand out against a white background. Medallions with cupids and scenes of the grape harvest can also be seen.

topographical references, such as the cemetery "of the two laurels". The third group is named after saints, and mostly acquired their names after the official recognition of Christianity in the fourth century: Sant'Agnese, San Pancrazio. A final group consists of anonymous cemeteries that archaeologists have named after the place of their discovery: Santa Croce Catacomb, New Via Latina Catacomb. Clearly, personal names are rarer than topographical references.

Many mausoleums, both pagan and Christian, cluster around the gates of Rome. These were the highest expression of funerary architecture in the empire. They were usually circular or polygonal in plan, and enclose monumental tombs. The mausoleum of Constantina on the Via Nomentana dates from early in the second quarter of the fourth century; it has a circular plan with annular ambulatory, whose vaults are decorated with mosaics representing plant and geometric motifs, accompanied by portraits and depictions of agricultural activities.

The dome of the mausoleum of Centcelles, not far from Tarragona, is almost contemporary. It displays pagan and Christian themes executed in mosaic. Beside the scenes from the Old and New Testaments are personifications of the four seasons in the form of nude cupids alternating with throned figures. There is also a hunting scene presided over by the owner of the villa in which the mausoleum was found; this is probably the man commemorated.

The deceased and his or her memory are the central elements around which funerary architecture was organized. The portrait of the deceased, sometimes accompanied by several members of the family, is an essential element of the iconography of sculpted sarcophagi and often constitutes the central painted or mosaic decoration of the large mausoleums.

Architecture enriched with sculpture
Detail of the arcades of the mausoleum of Santa Costanza, Rome. Twelve identical pairs of columns separate the main room from the annular aisle. They bear composite capitals crowned with large cushion-shaped abaci, on which the semicircular arches rest.

The Mausoleum-
Martyrium

The imperial mausoleum
Mausoleum of Santa Costanza, interior view from the annular aisle. The central colonnade supports a wall pierced with windows that carries the dome. With its balanced proportions and finely detailed decoration, this edifice, intended for the daughter of Emperor Constantine, is in direct line of descent from more ancient Roman funerary domes. Its dome raised on a drum is clearly visible from the exterior.

The term "mausoleum" comes from the monumental tomb built in Halicarnassus in 377–353 B.C., by one of the king's of Asia Minor, Mausolus. Celebrated artists worked on their buildings, and it was reckoned one of the seven wonders of the world. It is thought that the structure was square, with a high base from which rose a pyramid crowned by a quadriga and statues of monarchs. In paleo-Christian architecture, the term "mausoleum" designates monumental tombs.

The mausoleum of the Church of the Nativity in Bethlehem was built at the behest of the Emperor Constantine on top of the site of the grotto of the Nativity. Octagonal in plan, it enclosed a large circular opening raised above the center of a floor richly decorated with mosaics. It must have been illuminated by an opening let into the pyramidal roof. The plan of the edifice reflects the functions of the principal parts. The forecourt offered pilgrims a place to rest and merchants a place to do business. The mausoleum proper, run by clerics who lived on the premises, also served as a *martyrium,* in memory of Christ's birthplace. The place where Christ was thought to have been born could be perceived through the opening cut into the ceiling of the grotto. (However, entry to the sacred grotto must originally have been effected from in front of the octagon.) The opening in the roof (*opaion*) and the opening in the ground linked the earth on which Christ was born and the sky to which He ascended some three decades later. Before and after services, the worshipper, especially the pilgrim, could walk around the inside of the mausoleum and look down through the grille into the grotto. Though the mausoleum-martyrium was connected to the basilica, the two structures visibly served different functions simultaneously, like Saint Peter's in Rome.

The rotunda of Anastasis on Golgotha was another of Constantine's undertakings. Constantine's mother, Helena, in 325 identified a rock-cut tomb in the heart of Roman Jerusalem as Christ's sepulcher. Constantine sent an imperial order to the Bishop of Jerusalem directing him to build there "a basilica more beautiful than any other". Begun in 325–326, the basilica, which also served as *martyrium,* was consecrated in 336. Mass was celebrated between the different locations, with processions leading from the basilica to the Rock of Calvary, the Holy Sepulcher, and behind the basilica to the *martyrium.* The entire complex symbolized and evoked the martyrdom of Christ, His sacrifice and Resurrection.

The mausoleum was generally arranged around a center, in a radial plan whose many variations depended on the uses to which each monument was put. An octagonal structure was often chosen for the grandiose imperial mausoleums of Late Antiquity. Diocletian's mausoleum in Split, for example, has an octagonal exterior and a circular interior, and is crowned by a hemispherical dome.

In general, the great mausoleums of Late Antiquity were not exclusively tombs. They often boasted two levels: the tomb was located either on the lower level or in a crypt; the upper served as a place of meditation, tranquillity and worship. The mausoleum or *martyrium* was sometimes commemorative, like the *heroa* (temple or shrine of a hero) built in memory of deceased emperors. The Pantheon in Rome was often imitated, especially for its circular plan, many internal niches, high dome, and general architectural vocabulary.

The mausoleum-*martyrium* sometimes adjoined the Christian basilica, and might even share its ornamental themes. It frequently adjoined the side of the church porch. The mausoleum of Helena, for example, was physically co-erected to the basilica of Marcellino e Pietro. In the desire to commemorate the Passion of Christ on a monumental scale, the design of the imperial mausoleum was transported to become a commemorative building symbolic of the Passion. The central plan then became the basic element of all churches commemorating the life of Christ and the Passion. The entry via the basilica drew the faithful toward the *heroon-martyrium,* which preserved the evidence of Christ's presence on earth. Many subsequent monumental Christian tombs adopted this architectural form.

THE CHRISTIAN AFFIRMATION

Aspects of Early Christian Architecture

The building of churches replaced the construction of public edifices in ancient society. The members of the ruling classes who had converted to Christianity became the patrons of these new buildings, just as their predecessors had subsidized the erection of temples, baths, and theaters. Following the example of Constantine, emperors, or senior functionaries acting in their name, became the primary benefactors of the most noted basilicas.

The bishops, at the heart of the ecclesiastical hierarchy, played a major role in the establishment of new houses of Christian worship. Amid the decoration of a basilican apse, it was usual to find episcopal representations or inscriptions that recalled the presence of the bishop as the head of the community and his role in the decision to undertake the construction or reconstruction of the building. At Ravenna, the mosaics of the church of San Vitale have preserved the memory of two bishops of the sixth century associated with the building of this venerated monument. Ecclesius (522–532) initiated the construction of a church inspired by the most prestigious monuments of Constantinople. On the mosaic in the back of the main apse, he is seen holding the maquette of the building in his draped hands as he offers it to Christ. He had commissioned the construction, but died just as the decoration was being carried out, before it was complete. This earned him his place in the mosaic, accompanied by angels and Saint Vitalis, who supports Christ in Glory.

Bishop Maximianus, who consecrated the monument, is also depicted standing next to the Emperor Justinian in a mosaic lower down and closer to the apse. The images of the two bishops are not accompanied by that of the banker Iulianus who, though he financed the entire construction, is known to us only through inscriptions. These have been interpreted as evidence of the financing of major religious enterprises by laymen. Whatever the truth of this, final authority rested with the bishops.

When we come to define the architecture and symbology of the basilica, the common elements are more important than the variations. There were many variations, but it is difficult to present an ordered, chronological account of the development of basilicas in any given region because the typology was so strong.

Forms of the Basilica from Rome to Milan

One of the unifying elements is the symbolic association of the basilica and the longitudinal plan. Although cupolas had greater prestige, the majority of church roofs were supported on timber frames. From the outside, the roofs of buildings with side-aisles displayed a characteristic shape created by the two inclined places that covered the central nave, forming a saddleback roof; simple pitched roofs covered the aisles.

Throughout the Roman west, ground-plans corresponded to two or three main formulas. The most common emphasized the east-west axis without neglecting the north-south axis. These buildings are said to have a basilical plan, although it would be more precise to use the term longitudinal plan. The entire construction formed a

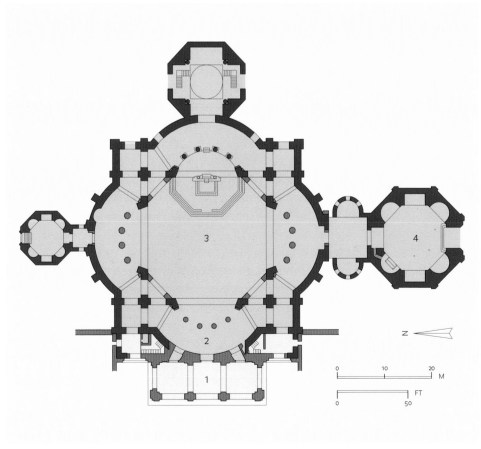

The narthex, a standard feature of the Christian basilica
San Lorenzo, Milan, exterior view from the *atrium,* end of the fourth century. This basilica with central dome, high tribune, and four square towers at its ends shelters imperial tombs, as well as those of many bishops of Milan. It is preceded by a huge atrium bordered by a colonnade of imposing proportions.

An exceptional example of a central-plan Christian church
San Lorenzo, Milan, plan, end of the fourth century. Tetraconch with dome, connected to poly-lobe chapels dedicated to Saints Aquilinus, Hippolytus, and Sixtus. The interior space presents a central core surrounded by a quatrilobe aisle.

1 Narthex
2 Quadrilobe aisle
3 Central room
4 Chapel of Sant' Aquilino

An auspicious place for triumphal theophanies
Mosaic of an absidiole of San Lorenzo, Milan, end of the fourth century. In the earliest Christian basilicas, the main apse was the place most often chosen to present synthetic theophanies that developed the visionary theme of Christ in Majesty.

rectangle with one of the short sides ending in an apse or, in exceptional cases, several apses. The upper walls of the nave bore the weight of the roof and rested on columns or pillars that separated it from the aisles. In structures without aisles, the timber roof rested on the top of the nave wall. Where a transverse nave, or transept, was built, its intersection with the nave was emphasized by a triumphal arch giving on to the apse.

Where in the longitudinal basilica the main axes determined the orientation and organization of the edifice, another type of structure made use of curvilinear elements. These edifices had a central plan, either circular or polygonal in shape. Making use of an architectural form characteristic of the Roman era, these structures might feature an ambulatory; a simpler type had no internal divisions. In the latter case, the roof rested directly on the walls.

In this brief survey of the most common of the main western forms, we shall limit ourselves to listing three types of central plan church. The first was multilobed churches having three semicircular apses opening from a square core, following a triconchos cruciform scheme, or a longitudinal plan ending in the same form. In the latter case, the triconchos was replaced by a single apse, which might be combined with the rounding of the two short arms of the transept. The second type, called mixed, combines and juxtaposes different formulas within the same structural plan. One of the best examples of this is the church of San Lorenzo in Milan, built toward the middle of the fourth century, which presents the fusion of a square plan and a triconchos preceded by an *atrium* and completed by a certain number of other external forms grafted onto the central core. Finally, the third and perhaps most prestigious type was cruciform churches; these fall into two groups, depending on

Sculpted capitals complete the didactic decoration
Detail of a capital in Sant' Ambrogio, Milan, end of the fourth century. Medieval Romanesque capitals draw on those of Late Antiquity. In this example the animal heads face away from a cruciform motif.

Page 47
The *atrium* enhances the façade of the Christian basilica
Façade of Sant'Ambrogio, Milan, end of the fourth century. This façade, evokes the monumental aspect of the great basilicas of Late Antiquity, and is characteristic of the monumental Romanesque of northern Italy.

whether the cross is free, i.e. visible from without, or enclosed within perimeter walls.

In Italy, the Constantinian tradition of prestige architecture endured in cities that sought to make their civil and religious architecture representative of power. Milan boasted particularly interesting examples of this tendency. At the end of the fourth century, among Milan's many churches, San Lorenzo Maggiore was perhaps the most original. It still stands; its central plan – a quatrefoil with ambulatory – is on two storeys, with high galleries surmounted by a dome (reconstructed in the sixteenth century). Four wide, square towers stand at its corners, and it was entered through a great square atrium. Sant'Ambrogio was also given a central plan, but its dimensions confer on it a quite exceptional character. On the other hand, the Latin cross basilical plan of the Basilica Apostolorum in Milan with small facing absidioles on the arms of the transept later reappeared in northern Italy, notably in Sant' Abbondio in Como, Santa Croce in Ravenna, Santo Stefano in Verona, and, with truly monumental proportions, San Simpliziano in Milan. Among Milan's highly varied architectural structures are some more traditional solutions, such as San Giovanni in

Conca, a nave without side-aisles ending in an apse, or the cathedral, with double-aisled nave and nonprojecting transept.

In Rome, paleo-Christian architecture matured during the period when the catacombs were abandoned and the bodies of martyrs transferred to churches *intra muros*. The architectural evolution of the fourth and fifth centuries is linear. The models of old Saint Peter's or San Giovanni in Laterano can, for example, be seen in San Paolo fuori le Mura, constructed about 385. From the fifth century, with the development of the cult of the Virgin and the martyrs, large churches were built on prestigious and symbolic sites, the best example being Santa Maria Maggiore on the Esquiline Hill. Begun by Pope Sixtus III (432–440), and continued by his successors until about 475, this basilica features nave and flanking aisles with integrated transept and an axial apse. At that time, papal involvement was decisive in forming the new religious architecture of Rome, in which churches or edifices with central

A veritable papal citadel
San Giovanni in Laterano, Rome,
plan:
1   Huge narthex with five openings
2   Basilica with nave and four aisles
3   Deep apse

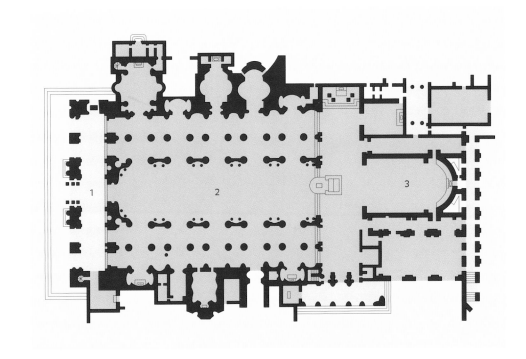

**The cross, symbol of
Christ's victory**
San Giovanni in Laterano, Rome,
interior view of the apse.
Triumphal arch and apsidal recess
were the spaces reserved for
the definition of doctrine. Here,
the cross stands out against the
sky and gives rise to the four rivers
of paradise at which deer come
to drink.

plans played a new role. The baptistery of San Giovanni in Laterano or the church of Santo Stefano Rotondo exemplify this trend with their annular ambulatories.

The lower church of San Clemente, better known since publication of its excavation, as Sant'Anastasia, Sant'Agata dei Goti, Santa Pudenziana, and the basilica of SS. Giovanni e Paolo present perfect examples of Roman architecture of the fifth century: the relatively narrow naves have gained in length and in height; the large arcades have multiplied; and the paleo-Christian *atrium* has everywhere been replaced by a narthex. Santa Sabina on the Aventine, erected between 422 and 432, perfectly defines the characteristics of the fifth-century basilica. It served as a model for other Roman basilicas of the fifth century and was imitated throughout the Middle Ages. A central nave flanked by aisles separated by arcades, leads toward a single, high semicircular apse. Its elevated position on the Aventine hill contributed to its archetypal image.

The baptistery, indispensable adjunct to the cathedral
San Giovanni in Laterano, Rome, exterior view of the baptistery. The marvelous Constantinian baptistery of the Lateran echoes the central-plan Roman mausoleums in its elevation (here polygonal).

Page 51
The baptismal vessel
San Giovanni in Laterano, Rome, interior view of the baptistery. The interior volumes, emphasized here by the later decoration, contribute to the solemn effect induced by the central space of the edifice, which houses the baptismal font.

The Originality of Ravenna

Rome and Milan were focuses of architectural attention for the rest of Italy. The influence of these centers on the religious architecture of northern Italy was considerable, from Verona to Brescia, Vicenza, and Pavia. The geographic location of the city of Ravenna, on the other hand, favored the interpenetration of Eastern and Western models, through the Adriatic and the Mediterranean.

Today, Ravenna is some 12 km from the Adriatic, lying south of Venice and east of Bologna. During Late Antiquity, however, it was somewhat closer to the sea and the port of Classe. The latter, situated about 3 km southwest of Ravenna, was built during the reign of Augustus. An impression of its appearance during Late Antiquity has been preserved by a mosaic in the church of Sant'Apollinare Nuovo. The Christian community of the old city, which was probably founded by Apollinare, was based in Classe until the transfer of the episcopal see to Ravenna at the end of the fourth century. Bishop Urso then built the new cathedral on the edge of the Roman city.

Some years later, in 402, Emperor Flavius Honorius moved the western capital from Milan to Ravenna; it offered, he felt, greater security from the threat of Alaric's Visigoths, and facilitated trade with the East. The city entered a resplendent phase under Galla Placidia, the half-sister of Honorius and regent during the childhood of Valentinian III (425–450). The location of the imperial palace remains controversial: was it near Santa Croce or between San Giovanni Evangelista and Sant'Apollinare Nuovo? The church of San Giovanni Evangelista dates from this period. It follows the usual northern Adriatic model in having a basilical plan and a wide nave, which extends into a semicircular apse enclosed in a polygonal external wall. Alongside the apse are two smaller spaces extending forward from the side-

The porticoed courtyard of antiquity was a feature of church architecture throughout the Middle Ages
San Clemente, Rome, view of the *atrium*. The *atrium* of paleo-Christian basilicas was a descendent of the porticoed courtyard of Roman houses. It was retained for the medieval basilicas of Rome, unchanged in internal and external appearance.

The ambo enriched the church furniture
San Clemente, Rome, interior. The ambo, or pulpit, is a marble construction that allows the clergy to speak to the congregation without leaving the liturgical space reserved for them.

In Rome, ancient Christian buildings were replaced by later structures
San Clemente, Rome, view of the lower basilica. The church of San Clemente, built in the Romanesque period, rests on earlier edifices, that is, the first basilicas built on the site, and these can be visited on San Clemente's lower level.

Light, an essential element of the basilica
Santa Sabina, Rome, interior, 422–432. The generous central space, covered with a timber roof above the ceiling, is extended by a prominent apse. The abundant light streaming in from the high windows and the revetment of polychrome marble on the arcades contribute to the harmony of the interior. This church served as a model for the basilicas built in Rome during the fifth century.

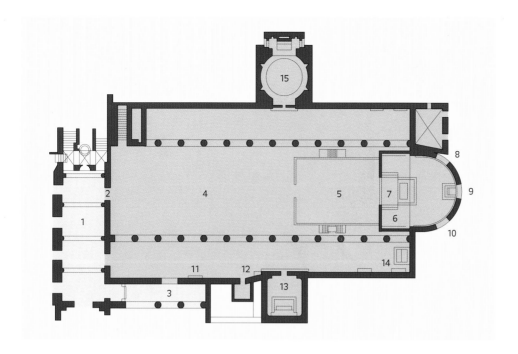

Side chapels added over the centuries
Santa Sabina, Rome, plan, 422–432. A nave and two aisles of even proportions, separated by twenty-four columns, lead to a very deep semicircular apse.
1 *Atrium*
2 Axial door
3 Side porch
4 Basilica with nave and two aisles
5 *Schola cantorum*
7 Pulpit
8 Apse window
9 Apse window
10 Apse window
11 Tomb of Bichi
12 Ancient column emerging from below right aisle
13 Chapel of Saint Hyacinth
14 Tomb of Cardinal Auxias de Podio
15 Chapel of Saint Catherine

Italian wooden sculpture from the early fifth century
Wooden entrance door of Santa Sabina, Rome, 422–432. It illustrates historic and symbolic subjects, as well as scenes from the two Testaments, inspired by the art of the catacombs, sarcophagi, and classical art. The most famous image is that of the Crucifixion: it is one of the earliest representations of Jesus in the crucified position. This door is an important example of Italian wooden sculpture of this period.

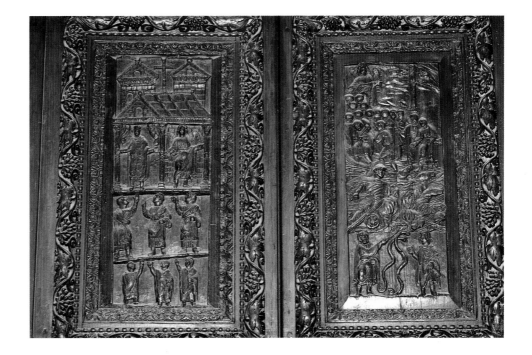

aisles. The church of Santa Croce was, for obvious reason, cruciform in plan. It has not survived. In the shadow of its portico stood the famous chapel known as the mausoleum of Galla Placidia. Known for its mosaic murals, it has a central plan in the shape of a Greek cross, with arms of equal length, and is crowned with a central dome. Its brick masonry is characteristic of Ravenna architecture of that period. Other notable churches are San Francesco, originally consecrated to the Holy Apostles, and Sant'Agata.

Gaul

Not far from Italy, the cathedral of Geneva has been the subject of exhaustive archaeological excavations which have revealed the characteristics of the first Christian edifices and their outbuildings. The effort to put together an atlas of the earliest Christian monuments in Gaul has produced a good number of new findings over the last few years. In urban as in rural milieux, it sometimes happened that the paleo-Christian sanctuary was built over the site of an ancient construction: in the open forum, as in Aix-en-Provence, or by integrating *thermae* as in Cimiez. In Metz, the church of Saint-Pierre-aux-Nonnains may have replaced a more ancient meeting hall. Finally, in some cases, as in Nîmes, the church simply occupied a classical temple.

Most of the Christian buildings in Gaul had a nave with side aisles or simply a nave. Aside from funerary structures, such as Saint-Laurent in Grenoble, the cruciform plan, normally created by the presence of a transept, is found in Saint-Laurent in Aosta and especially in buildings whose original states have long been a matter of controversy, such as Clermont, Nantes, and perhaps Tours, Lyons, and Narbonne. The church of Saint-Just in Lyons, whose second state may have been the mid-fifth-century basilica described by Sidonius Apollinaris in 469, presents a transept cross of square plan and, on either side of the apse, two rectangular compartments. Largely reconstructed, the church of Saint-Laurent-de-Choulans at Lyons also possessed a transept. The T-shaped plan, that is, with flat east end, single nave, and crossing level with the east end, was widespread in Alpine Gaul and in Germany.

Southern Gaul also possessed many very early Christian monuments: the baptisteries of Provence, the earliest of which date from the fifth century are identical to those of Italy. They are modeled on the "paleo-Christian" architecture of Italy.

**The *ciborium* of a
polygonal baptistery**
Reconstruction of the baptistery
of Mariana, Corsica. This cruciform church had a central baptismal font, also cross-shaped.
It was surrounded by a polygonal
baldachin or *ciborium,* as evi-
denced by the discovery of
sculpted fragments of small
columns and architraves. The
whole was richly decorated with
a mosaic floor on the theme of
water, which can be dated to the
beginning of the fifth century.

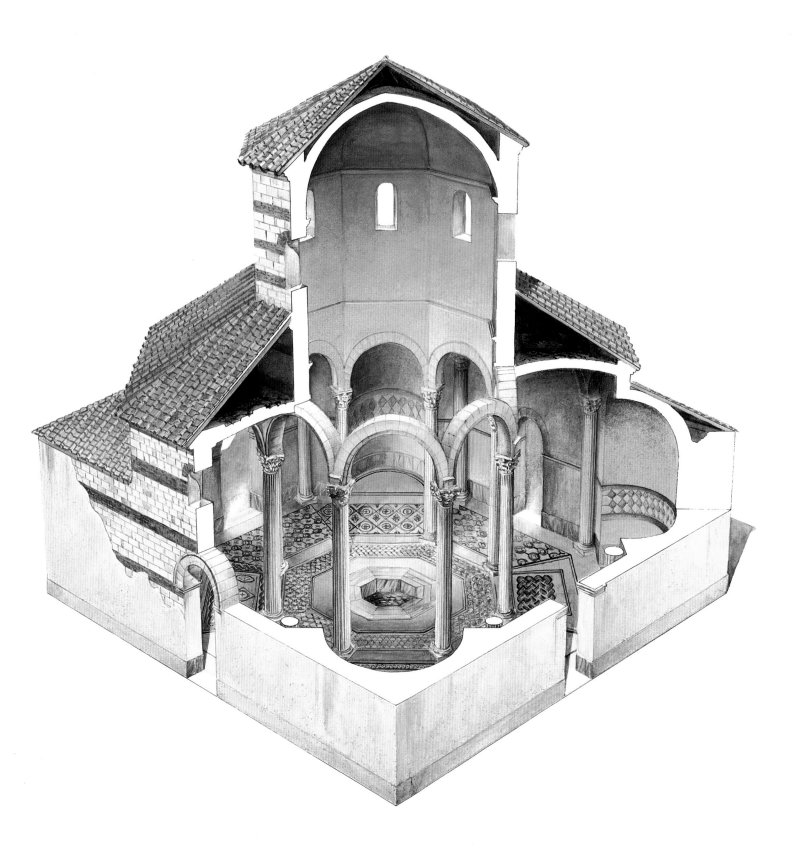

The prestige of the baptistery
Reconstruction of the baptistery of Marseilles, end of the fourth century. This structure, whose monumentality influenced all the other baptisteries of southern France, was an octagon, the intersection of whose arches was emphasized by the columns set on square bases. It had a circular ambulatory and drum. The baptismal font in the center is also octagonal.

**The baptistery:
a distinct architectural form**
Baptistery of Fréjus, Var, exterior,
beginning of the fifth century.
This structure, an octagon on a
square base, is set apart from
other Provençal baptisteries by its
lack of an ambulatory. It is distinguished from the medieval constructions around it by the ample
illumination of its polygonal drum.

The verticality of the baptistery
Baptistery of Fréjus, Var, cross
section, beginning of the fifth
century. Characteristic elevation
of a baptistery, here with an
interior decoration of veneered
arcades.

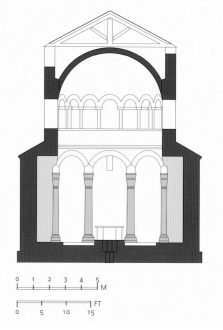

Their polygonal structures, built around a polygonal baptismal font, find expression
in a raised central body surmounted by a dome that symbolically protects the font
and serves as a monumental baldachin. Some baptisteries, such as those of Marseilles and Aix-en-Provence, have an ambulatory, while that of Fréjus, for example,
displays a simpler structure.

Page 61
**An architecture designed
around the baptismal font**
Above: Baptistery of Fréjus, Var,
interior view of the dome, beginning of the fifth century. Rebuilt
by J. Formigé, the dome allows a
recovery of the monumental
effect of the interior volume.
Below: Baptistery of Fréjus, Var,
interior, beginning of the fifth
century. The eight sides are ornamented with niches alternately
semicircular and rectangular, and
enriched with monolithic columns
of gray granite, crowned by white
marble capitals, most of them
from an earlier period.

The Other Ecclesiastical Building

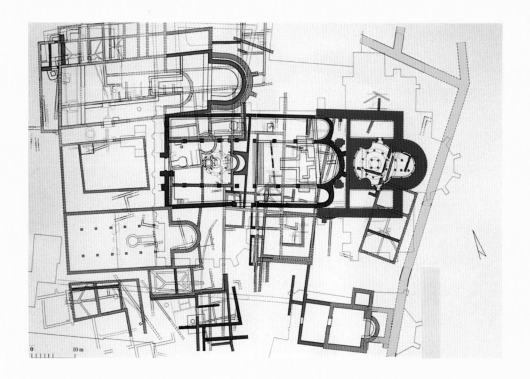

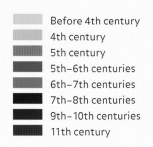

Archaeological excavation beneath a medieval cathedral
Episcopal group, Geneva, Switzerland, overall plan of excavations. This episcopal group was originally composed of two churches set parallel, separated by a baptistery to the east and an *atrium* at the west. The sixth-century cathedral came next, followed by those of the Romanesque and Gothic periods.

	Before 4th century
	4th century
	5th century
	5th–6th centuries
	6th–7th centuries
	7th–8th centuries
	9th–10th centuries
	11th century

Before the construction of the first basilicas, the early Christians gathered in premises called *domus ecclesiae.* Since then, the term has designated, not only a church, but the building or buildings erected near the cathedral to house the clerics and bishop and the staff attached to the main seat of the monastic community. Archaeologists have often overlooked these dwellings, but recent excavations and archive materials have provided a clearer picture of the *domus ecclesiae.* Gregory of Tours defined the *domus ecclesiae* as the bishop's residence. The bishop had his own room, the *cubiculum,* and after his death, his bed sometimes became a relic of miraculous properties. The *domus ecclesiae* also contained a refectory where the clergy ate communal meals, and a larger room in which the bishop could receive visitors. At Saint-Martin of Tours and Clermont-Ferrand, the texts speak of a *salutatorium.* This seems to have been a vast reception room. Charles Bonnet has identified a rectangular room with underheated mosaic floor, discovered in Geneva, as a *salvatorium,* but this cannot be confirmed. Excavations at Rouen Cathedral have brought to light a room with an apse that seems to be the *triclinium,* or bishop's reception room. Next to it were heated rooms, very likely a bath complex. It is, after all, logical that these ecclesiastical complexes would possess a traditional or simplified bath complex, such as those found in the Byzantine period.

The *domus ecclesiae* was thus in principle very like an aristocratic residence of the period. Some also contained an *oratorium,* an oratory or private chapel with altar and relics. These oratories gave rise to the episcopal chapels of the Middle Ages.

From the fourth century on, the episcopal residence was the principal for dispensing charity to the poor. This required the existence of premises for the distribution of food and clothing. Pilgrims and needy travelers could seek refuge in the residence, and the enormous room discovered in Poitiers, which seems to have been a hostel, may have served this purpose.

Finally, libraries, seminaries and schools are sometimes found in these complexes, as the *domus ecclesiae* was the site of an early form of semicommunal eternal life.

Episcopal groups are often double churches
Reconstruction of an episcopal group in Geneva, Switzerland. The principal church, which became the Gothic cathedral now standing, was built from the axial baptistery. A common *atrium* connected it with the southern church, which became a chapel dedicated to the Maccabees. (Watercolor drawing: Service cantonal d'Archéologie, Geneva)

From paganism to Christianity
Vestiges of the Christian basilica of Maktar, Tunisia, constructed in the fourth or fifth century re-using Roman elements. In this edifice with nave and two aisles and narthex, the columns, formerly placed outside, were arranged in the interior of the sanctuary, which from then on accommodated Christian worshippers.

From Spain to Africa

In other regions of the empire, the new Christian architecture followed paths similar to that taken in Italy. On the Iberian Peninsula, the introduction of new Christian monuments inside the walls of the city wrought changes in the urban fabric of the Roman city. The restoration of classical public buildings, such as the circuses of Mérida and Toledo, is an indication of urban continuity. It was rare for Christian monuments to replace pagan public edifices. Instead, they were located wherever building land was most accessible. Tarragona seems to have been an exception; there the implantation of the new religion assumed a symbolic aspect, with the construction of the cathedral opposite the classical forum in the main part of the city.

In the fourth century, Barcelona possessed richly decorated houses, one of which sported a floor mosaic representing the races at the circus, and the recently discovered *domus,* whose walls bear images of horsemen, suggests the continuity of the urban line; this is confirmed by archaeological excavations and the traces of monuments around the classical forum. It was formerly thought that the remains discovered in 1945 beneath the present cathedral, close to the city wall, were those of the first paleo-Christian cathedral, or perhaps of the famous basilica of Santa Cruz; in the latter, Paulinus of Nola informs us, a Synod was held in 599. It has recently been shown, that the site of the oldest episcopal basilica must be sought elsewhere, on the other side of the magnificent baptistery discovered in 1968. The latter was a square building containing a baptismal *piscina.* The *piscina* was originally cruciform in shape; later this was altered to an octagon. It stood at the center of an ambulatory and numerous annexes. The baptistery was very probably located at the east end of the paleo-Christian mother-church, probably accompanied by an episcopal complex, as at Terrassa.

Extensive funerary decoration in a private building

Mausoleum of Centcelles, Tarragona, interior view of fourth-century dome. Constructed in brick, the dome is decorated with concentric registers of mosaics, bringing together profane themes, such as the seasons, and biblical themes from the Old and New Testaments. The first register is given over to hunting.

Magnificence of an urban mausoleum

Villa and mausoleum of Cent-celles, Tarragona, plan. Situated in the heart of a suburban villa, the mausoleum includes two central-plan rooms, integrated into a single rectangular building. It exemplifies both the artistic accomplishment available to the great courtier-landowners of the mid-fourth century and the splendor with which they endowed their last resting-places.

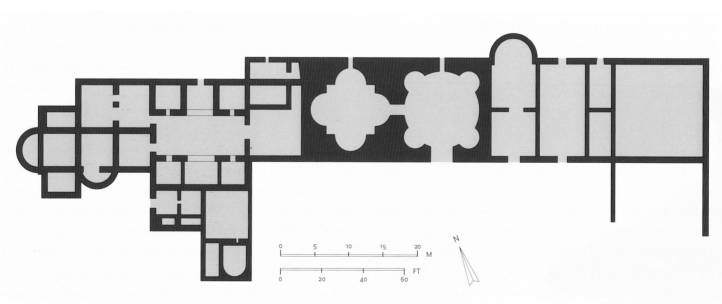

Mosaics cover the floor and font of the baptistery
Baptismal font in Sbeïtla, Tunisia. The floor mosaic covers both floor and font. The steps on the short sides are for entering and leaving the font.

In Egara (present-day Terrassa), three buildings have survived of the episcopal complex, to which we shall return in a later chapter. Earlier excavations yielded buildings dating from the middle of the fifth century, which was when the diocese of Barcelona was divided; Irenaeus was made the first bishop of Egara in 450. Among the discoveries was a church without aisles, with a trapezoidal apse at its east end and a lateral funerary chamber. A baptistery was located behind the apse of this church, but in the seventh century it made way for a church with nave and flanking aisles. This in its turn was replaced by the medieval buildings visible today.

Tarragona was the central metropolis of the region and an important city during Late Antiquity; much archaeological research remains to be done there. Although the site of the old cathedral has not yet been located, several funerary churches have been unearthed. One of these was consecrated to Saint Fructuosus; its nave and flanking aisles (it probably possessed a transept), semicircular apse, and two lateral rooms, were long unearthed in an enormous zone of necropolises, in which the remains of a paleo-Christian basilica have recently been discovered.

The oldest Christian necropolises, like those of Francoli in Tarragona, Cartagena, Córdoba, or Gerona, have yielded sculpted sarcophagi. These are no less revealing than architecture of the taste of those who commissioned them in the fourth century. Many of these sarcophagi were imported from Rome. Imported sarcophagi have been found at Astorga, Córdoba, Martos, and San Felíu de Girona in Catalonia, all of them from the early fourth century. Later examples include those in the cathedral of Tarragona, and the sarcophagi embellished with strigils in the museum of Valencia. Where figures are carved on them, the iconography, draws equally on the Old and New Testaments, and reflects a concern with the theme of Salvation. Some of the wealthier patrons ordered sarcophagi from workshops in other provinces of the empire, importing them from, for example, North Africa (some of the sarcophagi in Tarragona originally came from Tunisia) or Aquitania. Several groups of sarcophagi came from local workshops, like that of Bureba in the Burgos region.

Among the most important paleo-Christian monuments of Spain is the mausoleum of Centcelles, built at the end of the first third of the fourth century, not far from Tarragona. Part of a large suburban villa, this structure is crowned with a dome decorated with mosaics representing a large hunting scene presided over by the owner of the villa. The profane iconography is juxtaposed with scenes from the Old and New Testaments in a clearly deliberate symbolism. The monument's architectural significance, its similarities with the mausoleum of Constantina in Rome, and the richness of its decoration have led to the hypothesis that it is the mausoleum of Constantine's son, Constantine II.

One of the main aspects of monumental decoration in Christian architecture was floor mosaics. In Spain, as elsewhere in the empire, such mosaics divide into two main types. The first and older type dates from the fourth and fifth centuries; it is found throughout the Mediterranean basin. Elche and Terrassa provide excellent examples of this style, in which the surface of the floor is covered with panels bearing geometric and plant motifs, and little room is left for figuration. The second type, dated closer to the sixth century, is particularly well represented in the Balearic Islands; it shows the influence of North Africa and of animal themes deriving from eastern iconography. To illustrate the work of a single workshop, an iconographical and stylistic comparison could be made between the floor-mosaics of the basilicas of Es Fornas de Torella and La Illeta del Rei in Menorca.

In terms of floor-plans, the churches of the Iberian Peninsula can be divided into three categories. The simplest presents an apse flanked by lateral rooms, the whole enclosed in a unifying rectangular outline. It is illustrated at Son Bou, Empuries, and Elche. The second derives from the first but features a second apse at the west end (Vega del Mar, Casa Herrera). The third type, illustrated by the basilica of Tarragona, has a central apse flanked by two free-standing lateral rooms.

On the other side of the Mediterranean, the many surviving paleo-Christian edifices of North Africa deserve an entire study to themselves. But that area falls outside the geographic scope of this book. The Romanized African coast, comprising several provinces, saw a flowering of Christian religious constructions in the period before the arrival of the Vandals in 430. At that time, old Roman monuments were frequently adapted to the needs of the new religion, as in Maktar. In Algeria and Tunisia, the most common form of basilica was extremely simple: a rectangular ground-plan twice as long as wide was oriented to the east and entered by the western façade. The majority featured a nave and two aisles, although some more important sanctuaries, such as those at Orléansville and Dermerch, near Carthage, had four aisles. An atrium often preceded the basilica, as at Tebessa or in the Donatist basilica at Timgad. Finally, there were many structures built to hold relics in their crypts. The most spectacular example of such a crypt is that of Djemila, in Algeria, where a subterranean corridor connects a series of underground apses to the monumental east ends of the two basilicas of the episcopal complex.

The Elements of the Basilica

The monumentality of the Christian basilica
Santi Cosma e Damiano, Rome, interior, 526–530. The imposing nave of the basilica magnifies the solemnity of the standing Christ that presides over the theophany of the apse. Despite later additions, the original volumes have been preserved.

For the Christians of Late Antiquity, the term "basilica" meant a building that was devoted to Eucharistic worship. This was a simple edifice, of rectangular or central plan and was primarily intended to accommodate those who had gathered for liturgical celebration. The authority of the basilican model became established under Constantine and went from strength to strength thereafter.

The orientation of basilicas followed certain set rules. (By orientation is meant the cardinal point indicated by the axis of the apse.) At first, no particular rule was observed, and the building was simply designed in accordance with the lay of the land. Some buildings were simply lined up with a sacred place, such as the tomb of a martyr. In the eighth century, orientation to the east became prevalent, and by the ninth century had become standard.

The paleo-Christian basilica was an architectural complex made up of different structures, each intended to serve a precise liturgical or social function. The classification of the religious community into different groups and the need to afford each category a particular space during the service led to the appearance of reserved areas. For example, the catechumens (those receiving instruction but not yet baptized and therefore debarred from communion) had to remain outside the church. Only the faithful could attend the Eucharistic rite. Of the forms of architecture devised to accommodate the catechumens at the churchdoor, the most common was the *atrium.* This was a large, open space surrounded on at least three sides by porticoes. Under Constantine, the basilica *atrium,* inspired by that of the

Roman house, began to spread through the Mediterranean basin. The exceptions were Syria and North Africa, where few examples can be found. The porticoes that surrounded the open courtyard formed a continuous covered ambulatory, sometimes on two storeys. The upper storey might be enclosed by a wall or open and colonnaded.

The narthex is a porch located in front of the façade. It can be transversal, and may be external or integral to the church. The narthex was initially intended to accommodate the catechumens and the penitents, who were not allowed to enter the religious edifice. In the seventh century, this very specific use disappeared; in its stead came other functions, such as petitions, and, in monasteries, the celebration of the service. In the medieval church, it was simply a porch.

The arrangement of the façade depended on whether there were one or three doors. Above the doors, a large, central window and sometimes two lateral openings provided light and symmetry. In buildings with a narthex or *atrium*, the monumental aspect of the façade was confined to the upper level, and its role was aesthetic rather than functional.

Inside the edifice, a nave and aisles divided the church; a series of columns or pilasters created smaller units, each with its own role. The similarity of the nave to an upturned hull – the word derives from the latin *navis* (ship) – reinforced the symbolism of the Church as ship. Nave and aisles almost always formed an uneven number between one and five; the tripartite system was most commonly used, with the central nave higher than the aisles. The nave and aisles in paleo-Christian basilicas were capped with a ceiling that concealed the timber rafters and a tile roof. Central-plan edifices often had a dome. The transverse nave of the basilica was called the transept, from *trans saepta,* "beyond the enclosure". It separated the nave (and aisles) from the choir, giving rise to the T or cross shape, symbolizing the Cross of Christ. The transept might be of the same width as the rest of the building or project beyond it.

The choir is the liturgical space that includes or precedes the main apse; it was used exclusively by the clergy during liturgical celebrations. It was sometimes higher than the nave to enhance its visibility. The choir is bound by chancels or other forms of enclosure, which assert the symbolic isolation of the sacred area. It comprises the apse, the altar, the *catedra* (bishop's throne) and seating for priests, the ambo, the chancels, and the crypt.

The altar, the focal point of the basilica, symbolizes the table of Christ's Last Supper and, recalling Golgotha, periodically repeats the sacrifice of the Cross. This twofold significance explains the variety of forms it took, among them table, sarcophagus and chest. The altar was also used to hold relics. It was covered by a *ciborium* or symbolic protection formed by a canopy supported on four columns which stood one on each side of the high altar. This evoked the roof of a tomb, the canopy of a throne, and the covering of the tabernacle.

The apse is the termination of the choir and the church. A feature of Roman public basilicas and the reception rooms of houses and palaces, in the paleo-Christian basilica the apse housed the *catedra,* or principal throne, situated in the curve of the apse and flanked by the *subsellia,* benches reserved for the priests (the deacons remained standing). The apse symbolizes the link between Church triumphant and Church militant constructed by the ecclesiastical hierarchy.

The crypt, situated beneath the choir, contained holy relics. The term originally designated a pit or a small, rectangular cell over which the altar was built. An architectonically defined crypt did not, however, develop until at least the sixth century; it became the nucleus of the medieval

**The unity of the apse
and the triumphal arch**
Mosaic of the apse of the Basilica
of Santi Cosma e Damiano, Rome,
526–530. The miraculous healers
from Persia, Damian and Cosmas,
the patron saints of physicians, are
led to heaven by Saint Peter and
Saint Paul and offer their crowns
to Christ, who appears standing in
front of the river of paradise.

Page 68
**Complementary architecture
and decoration**
Santa Prassede, Rome, interior
view of the chapel of Saint Zeno.
This mosaic underlines on the
one hand the continuity of the
iconography and, on the other,
the close connections between
architecture and decoration, most
strikingly in the figures that follow
the ribs of the vault.

basilica. The *pastoforae,* or absidioles, were small
spaces arranged along the sides of the apse or
choir with a role analogous to that of the side-
aisles. The *schola cantorum* was a rectangular
enclosure, often raised by one or two steps and
situated immediately in front of the choir, where
singers or clergy took their places during solemn
ceremonies. This space often adjoined the choir,
forming a single space bordered by the chancels.
It first appeared in the sixth century. The ambo, a
kind of pulpet where the priest read the holy
scriptures, gave the sermon, or announced celebrations, was not found in all basilicas.

The chancel served as an enclosure or, at
least, division between the area reserved for the
clergy and the nave, following liturgical and prac-
tical requirements. It was usually composed of
carved stone or marble flagstones or pillars.

Some Christian basilicas possessed a gallery
above the side-aisles; when this extended along
the inside wall of the façade, it was called a tribune. These galleries were as wide as the aisles but
lower; they opened onto the nave in bays divided
by columns or pilasters and protected by marble
parapets. The tribunes generally communicated
with the lower storey by a stairway located in the
narthex.

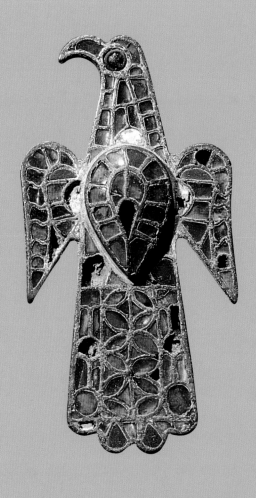

National Architecture

From Italy to Gaul

On 31 December 406, the Vandals, Alans and Sueves crossed the Rhine in the area of Mainz or Worms. After passing through Gaul, these peoples entered Spain, probably in October 409. After a period of war and raiding, they divided up the Iberian Peninsula in 411 or 412. Their role did not last long, however; the Alans had vanished by 418, wiped out by the Visigoths. The Vandals penetrated North Africa and formed a powerful state, which nevertheless proved vulnerable to the Byzantine expansion of the sixth century. Only the Sueves retained a portion of Lusitania and Galicia.

The Burgundii, whom the momentum of 406 had pushed into Lower Germany, had, by 413, obtained a *foedus* close to the Rhine but within the borders of Gaul. In 436, the Roman commander Aetius forced them to move further south, toward the area around Geneva, where they formed the First Kingdom of Burgundy, which stretched as far as Lyons and included southern Champagne and the maritime Alps. This state lasted until the end of the first third of the sixth century, when it was absorbed by the Franks.

The Visigoths under Athanulf approached Gaul from the east, before this, across Italy; their invasion of Gaul began in 412. Goths from the northeast of the Black Sea, along with other barbarian peoples had, after clashing with the Romans, crossed the Danube at the end of the third quarter of the fourth century. The Visigoths, led by Alaric, wandered in the Balkans for several years, arriving in Italy in 401. They besieged Milan and Aquileia until pressure from the Roman general Paulus Stilicho constrained Alarich to lift his siege, and he headed for Rome instead. He reached Rome by 408 but did not actually enter it until two years later, dying before he had attained his goal of invading North Africa. His successor, his brother-in-law Athanulf, resumed the road to the north and entered Gaul with his people; he took Narbonne, Toulouse, and Bordeaux in 413. In January 414, at Narbonne, he married Galla Placidia, whom he had captured in Rome. Her brother Honorius, the Emperor of Rome, opposed the marriage and forced Athanulf to withdraw to Barcelona, where he was assassinated. It was not until 418 that the Visigoths received from Honorius the right to establish themselves in Aquitania Secunda and certain districts of the Midi, a territory that included the cities of Bordeaux, Angoulême, Périgueux, Poitiers, and Toulouse.

A new danger compelled all the inhabitants of Gaul to concentrate their efforts on the northern front as the Huns, led by Attila, crossed the Rhine in their turn in 451 and took Metz on 7 April. They reached Orléans before being defeated by a double army organized by the Roman general Aetius and the Gothic leader Theodoric I in the famous battle of the Catalaunian Plains (Châlons-sur-Marne). Attila then turned towards Italy.

A period of territorial partition among these newcomers now began. The Franks, established on the Rhine and in the region of Cologne from the end of the fourth century, penetrated farther into Gaul during the second quarter of the fifth century. Though they took no part in the coming of the *limes* in 406 by the Alans and

Vandals, they took advantage of this movement and in due course founded the Merovingian dynasty. Childeric, who died in 481, began to consolidate their territory in north Gaul, and his son Clovis (481–511) extended this to the Pyrenees, aided by his victory at Vouillé over Alaric II's Visigoths in 507. The Merovingian dynasty, converted to Christianity, gave way to the Carolingians.

Pushed toward Spain, the Visigoths, who had established the capital of their kingdom in Toulouse, migrated first toward Narbonne and Barcelona before establishing their capital definitively in Toledo. Leowigild (568–586) controlled the majority of the peninsula, and his son Hermenegild, who converted to Christianity in 587, enhanced Toledo's religious and cultural status. Spain remained Visigothic until the Muslim advance in 711, when the Visigothic kingdom abruptly perished.

Italy, through which the Visigoths had passed, was conquered by another eastern people, the Ostrogoths, who had been subjugated by the Huns and had settled in Pannonia after having attacked Constantinople in 487. Zeno, the East Roman emperor, pushed the Ostrogoths back toward Italy after a period of uneasy alliance and a temporary settlement in Macedonia. The Ostrogoth king, Theodoric the Great, entered Italy in 489 and conquered the peninsula, defeating Odoacer (the first barbarian king of Italy) in 493. He made Ravenna his capital. After his death in 526, the Ostrogothic kingdom of Italy survived only until the Byzantine conquest undertaken by Justinian a few decades later.

The Merovingians in Gaul, the Visigoths in Hispania, and the Ostrogoths in Italy brought with them artistic traditions that found expression in metalwork and the decorative arts. Each of these peoples settled in strongly Romanized areas of the West that possessed a rich and abundant, classical and paleo-Christian architectural tradition. The combination of local building traditions, architectural mod-

The art of Visigothic metalwork
Visigothic belt buckle in bronze, sixth century. The motif of two facing animals across a bream from which plants of life spring echoes the age-old theme of animals framing a "Tree of Paradise". Here, however, the paleo-Christian figurative heritage is very much in evidence. (Museo Arqueológico Nacional, Madrid)

Page 75
The mausoleum, symbol of the prince
Mausoleum of Theodoric, Ravenna, exterior, end of the fifth century. It was built with large blocks of stone and has a polygonal plan and a two-story elevation capped with a monolithic dome. The upper story was intended to hold the royal sarcophagus, the lower presumably for religious or official functions.

els common throughout the empire, and the new artistic tendencies of the invaders gave rise to the first architectural forms in the West that can be considered national.

Italy

Ravenna remained a very important city under Odoacer, the king of Italy after the death of the last emperor in 476. The king of the Ostrogoths, Theodoric, defeated Odoacer in 493, but retained Ravenna as his capital, which it remained until his death in 526. The city's growth under his reign was marked by the construction of city walls whose extent was matched only by the splendor of Theodoric's new palace; this was built next to Sant'Apollinare and possessed a palatine chapel. An often disputed iconographic document provides some information about this palace: the mosaic of the church of Sant'Apollinare Nuovo, which shows a façade in three parts. Some believe it offers a schematic view of the porticoed ceremonial court of the palace; others see in it an exploded view of a basilica. In fact, the archaeological discoveries made at the site of the palace do not suggest the con-

struction of an entirely new palace; They seem, rather, to point to an older villa with a traditional plan, which Theodoric transformed to create his palace.

During the reign of the Ostrogoths, the architecture of Ravenna was considerably enriched. Monumental forms specific to Ravenna developed and the tradition of construction in brick became established. Thus, the Gothic kings built an Arian cathedral, the Basilica of Santo Spirito, with a baptistery whose architecture, like the mosaics that adorn the raised central section, are still in a state of excellent preservation today. Theodoric, seeking to emulate eastern grandeur and the mythical past of his predecessors, ordered the construction of a mausoleum highly original in both its plan and elevation. Unlike anything else in in Ravenna, the building is, nonetheless, an apt symbol of Theodoric's impact on the city: a rotunda built with huge blocks of ashlar, it is of polygonal plan, and its two-storey elevation is covered by a monolithic dome of extraordinary size. The lower level was probably used for religious purposes, while the circular upper storey contained the royal sarcophagus. The size of the blocks of stone and the vast monolith of its dome set this building quite apart from the architectural production of the period.

It is this first part of Ravenna's history – Late Antiquity and the Early Middle Ages – which constitutes the main focus of this volume. The city experienced a new burst of building after the defeat of the Goths and the city's conquest by the armies of Byzantium in 540. Under Justinian, the religious architecture of Ravenna flourished. To the existing churches of basilical plan was added San Vitale, with its central plan, annular ambulatory, and galleries. It was a model which had an immense impact on western medieval architecture, and on palatine churches in particular.

Along with Rome, Salonika, and Constantinople, Ravenna is a veritable museum of fifth- and sixth-century paleo-Christian religious architecture. The thick bricks used during the fifth century and the exteriors decorated with pilasters and shallow blind arcades give these buildings their distinctive appearance. The blind arcades

The richness of colors and quality of execution of the mosaics
Detail of the mosaic decoration from the main register of the left wall of the nave, Sant'Apollinare Nuovo, Ravenna, fifth century. The saints and virgins stand out against a gold background; in their hands, they hold crowns symbolizing martyrdom. The figures here represent, from left to right, Agnes, Agatha, Pelagia, and Euphemia. The work is based on a palette of gold, white, emerald, and jewelled tones; it uses dark outlining to emphasize shapes and tonalities.

Rhythm and proportions in a processional frieze

Detail of a mosaic decoration from the main register of the right wall of the nave, Sant'Apollinare Nuovo, Ravenna, fifth century. The train of martyrs moves toward the enthroned Christ. At the other end, near the entrance of the church, appears the palace of Theodoric. It presents a perfect example of the theme of the processional frieze, earlier treated in the sculptures of the Parthenon and the walls of the palaces of Assyria and Persia.

are reminiscent of the slightly earlier structures in Milan and Trier. A particularly noteworthy example is the so-called tomb of Galla Placidia. This small monument was, in fact, a chapel abutting the narthex of the basilica of Santa Croce, which no longer survives.Its cruciform plan features a central bay crowned with a flattened dome. The cruciform plan, here, a Latin cross, was also adopted in the basilica of Santa Croce, which was not dissimilar to San Simpliziano and the Basilica Apostolorum in Milan.

The basilical plan generally meant a nave and two side-aisles; one exception is the Duomo known as degli Ortodossi, which had two additional aisles. The proportions were very harmonious, following the western tradition of a nave twice as wide as the side-aisles. The apses, on the other hand, have more in common with the East and Constantinople, to the extent that, from the very beginning, they presented a polygonal external plan while retaining the semicircular Roman plan on the inside. The elevation is traditional, with the nave higher than the aisles and a timber roof. The nave is separated from the aisles by monolithic columns that support semicircular arches. There are large windows in the clerestory, the side-aisles and the back of the apse.

At the end of the sixth century, the Lombards from the north of Italy settled in cities for the most part already inhabited. They made use of the existing monuments, such as, for example, the palace of Pavia. Between the sixth and the eighth centuries, they built large churches in Pavia, Cividale (Santa Maria in Valle and San Martino), and Castelseprio (Santa Maria foris portas).

Merovingian Gaul

Study of the Christian topography of cities, analysis of urban and rural residences, original documents, and archaeological excavations have all contributed to our understanding of the monumental landscape of Gaul during Late Antiquity. Out-

Cruciform Christian mausoleum in the Roman tradition
Tomb of Galla Placidia, Ravenna, exterior, first half of the fifth century. This brick edifice, small in dimensions, has a cruciform plan with equal arms. It is crowned with a central dome. It was built at the end of the narthex of the church of Santa Croce, which has not survived.

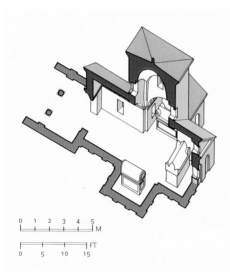

A compact structure
Axonometric projection of the Tomb of Galla Placidia, Ravenna, first half of the fifth century. This is the mausoleum of the daughter of Theodosius I, the sister of Honorius and mother of Valentinian III.

The cross in the firmament
Mosaic of the dome in the Tomb of Galla Placidia, Ravenna, first half of the fifth century. In the center, a gold cross stands out against a blue background sprinkled with stars. The symbols of the four Evangelists are represented in the pendentives.

Page 82
A sky of mosaics, stars, and scrollwork
Details of the mosaics in the Tomb of Galla Placidia, Ravenna, first half of the fifth century. The lunettes present scenes of female saints, figures of the apostles, the Good Shepherd, and deer drinking from the fountain of life. The martyrdom of Saint Lawrence occupies the main lunette. The ceiling is covered with a mosaic decoration of scrollwork, garlands, and geometric motifs from which the Chi-Rho, or Christogram, emerges.

**The sanctuary of
the bishops of Vienne**
Saint-Pierre, Vienne, exterior,
fifth–eleventh century. The early
church is a nave without aisles,
rectangular in shape, and flanked
in the east by a semicircular apse.
Built under the name of the Holy
Apostles, it houses the tombs of
numerous bishops of Vienne. The
Romanesque belfry is one of the
many pieces of rebuilding carried
out over the centuries.

Early basilica without aisles
Saint-Pierre, Vienne, plan, second
half of the fifth century. On the
inside the side walls of the nave
present two rows of seven double
arcades. To the north, the apse is
flanked by a rectangular addition
communicating with the nave.
To the south, the early structures
have been modified by the construction of a corridor connecting
Saint-Pierre with the Oratory of
Notre-Dame.
1 Nave
2 Veneered colonnade
3 Apse
4 Rectangular addition
5 Connecting corridor
6 Oratory of Notre-Dame

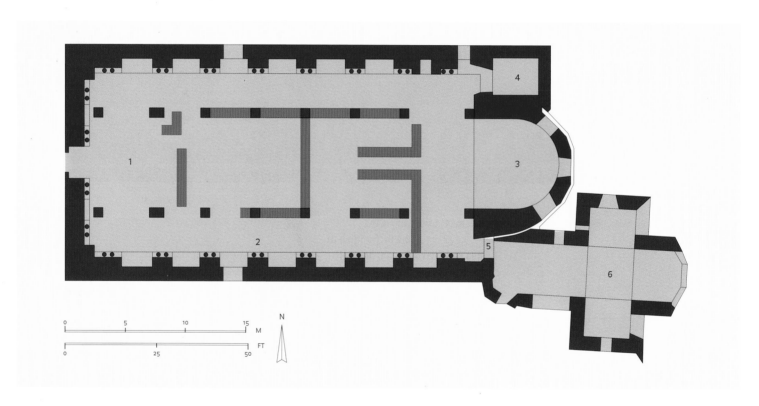

side the cities, necropolises and funerary basilicas arose near the tombs of martyrs
and local saints. Sidonius Apollinaris described the double cathedral of Lyons.
Basilican plans sometimes excluded side-aisles, as in Saint-Pierre in Vienne, the former basilica des Apôtres (fifth–sixth century) and sometimes included them, as in
Saint-Laurent in Lyons. In Toulouse, the fifth century basilica de la Daurade no
longer extant presented a semicircular plan with ambulatory and was decorated
with beautiful mosaics. Gregory of Tours described the basilica of Saint-Martin at
Tours as a small structure with side-aisles and galleries.

The city of Poitiers preserves two monuments essential to our understanding
of Merovingian architecture. The first stage of construction of the baptistery
dates back to the paleo-Christian era, when it must have stood next to the city's
cathedral. After numerous restorations, all that remains of the original rectangular
structure is perhaps the baptismal font, which cannot be earlier than the last years

Page 85
**Former arrangement
of the inner walls of the nave**
Saint-Pierre, Vienne, interior view
of the nave, fifth–eleventh
century. Columns separating the
three main spaces of this edifice,
which today serves as a lapidary
museum, probably date from the
Romanesque period. The two rows
of arcades of the inner walls of
the nave resting on small double
columns crowned with capitals
recall the superimposed orders of
the Late Roman Empire.

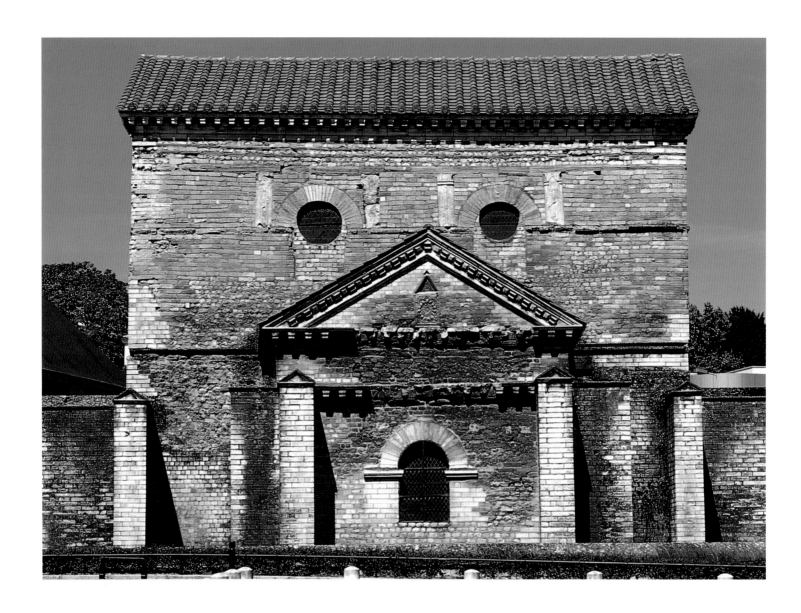

of the fourth century. The alternation of brick and stone, characteristic of Merovingian masonry, indicates a very substantial renovation of the baptistery and the entire complex; this took place around the middle of the seventh century. Inside, a high rectangular space was divided into two rooms, the more easterly of which was extended by the addition of two lateral outbuildings at its northern and southern ends. To the east, the apse is pentagonal inside and trapezoidal on the outside. Despite successive renovations of the outside walls, the different layers of masonry remain visible. Inside, the arcades frame the windows, imparting a rhythmic aspect to the walls; outside, the upper sections of the wall are ornamented with geometric motifs in brick. Today, the baptistery of Poitiers remains, despite the transformations of the Romanesque era, a repository of information about Merovingian architecture.

The hypogeum of Dunes is a funerary chapel from the Merovingian period located outside the city of Poitiers in a vast necropolis of classical origin which continued to be used during Late Antiquity. Though no mention of it is made in contemporary documents, this half-underground building is undoubtedly one of the most important western funerary monuments of the period. Inscriptions tell us that the tomb was built for an abbot named Mellebaude. The complex was discovered during the second half of the nineteenth century.

The monument is accessible by means of a stairway of about ten steps, which leads to a monumental door. A roughly rectangular space almost 5 m deep is enlarged by lateral *arcosolia* (shallow arched recesses). The ceiling vault was

Originality of stonework and exterior decoration
Saint-Jean, Poitiers, exterior views of the east (above) and the southwest façade (page 87 above) of the baptistery, seventh century. The façades present amid various moldings, small-scale, irregular stonework, then in regular stonework with a decoration of pilasters.

Page 87 below
A Merovingian baptistery
Saint-Jean, Poitiers, plan and reconstruction of the southwest façade. This baptistery shows a rectangular room extended at the east by a polygonal apse and furnished with two lateral absidioles.
1   Five-sided narthex
2   Baptismal chamber
3   Baptismal font
4   Lateral absidioles
5   Polygonal apse

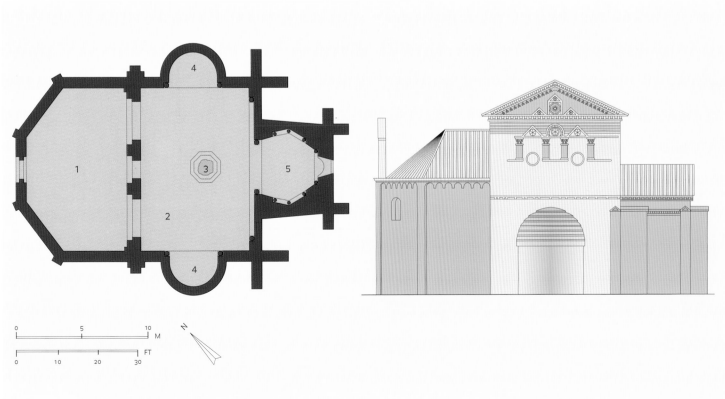

Page 88

Elevation from the Merovingian period and its reutilization in the Romanesque period

Saint-Jean, Poitiers, interior view toward the apse, seventh century. Arcades resting on marble columns decorate the walls of the apse and the baptismal chamber. The twelve columns of the upper parts, made of limestone and crowned with capitals bearing large leaves, echo the decoration of the external pilasters. A wealth of diverse materials characterizes this ornamentation.

Play of colors and recourse to various materials

Detail of the upper portion of the gable end, southwest wall, of Saint-Jean, Poitiers, seventh century. Above the *oculi* and a course supported by four pilasters, three small niches, one semicircular and two triangular, are ornamented with terracotta rosettes, as are the triangular niches in the pediment. An impressive cornice with modillions above a pelta motif emphasizes the slope of the roof. This decoration of alternating stone and brick offers a good example of Merovingian wall ornamentation.

probably protected by a timber roof. In the center of the raised section at the back of the rectangular space, a block of masonry supported the altar table. The five main sarcophagi were placed on the ground, along the walls, three in the *arcosolia*. Other sarcophagi surrounded the altar. The tomb is also famous for its painted decoration, architectural sculpture, carved sarcophagi, freestanding sculpture, and inscriptions.

This kind of funerary chapel is found in many cemeteries of the late Roman era, but the state of the Dunes *hypogeum* at the time of its discovery made it quite exceptional. The tradition to which it belongs is suggested by other, older examples, notably those in the paleo-Christian necropolises of Tarragona and Carthage. The Dunes hypogeum is a *cella memoriae* (memorial chamber) provided with everything required for worship. Here services could be held on certain dates and the tomb could thus be used as a funerary chapel. The situation of Abbot Mellebaude's tomb and that of the other sarcophagi is reminiscent of a family vault of the

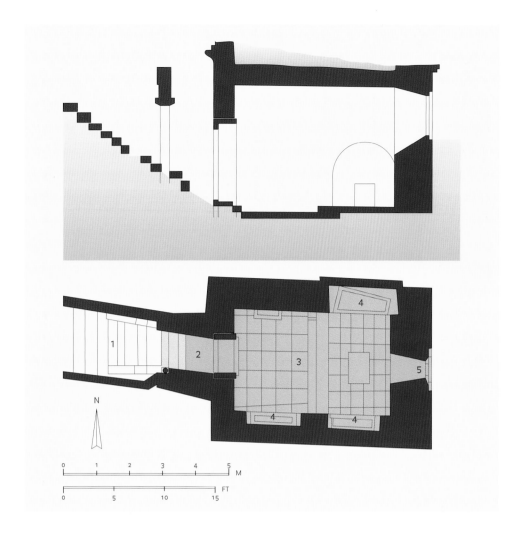

cubicula type in the catacombs. The style of the sculptures, the typology of the sarcophagi, and certain iconographic and epigraphic details date the monument to the late seventh century or the first third of the eighth.

In seventh-century Gaul, abbeys began to be established in the former large Gallo-Roman estates; earlier constructions were re-used, as in Jouarre in the valley of the Marne, Fleury, Moûtier-Grandval, and Nivelles. The state of preservation of these buildings means that we cannot identify an architectural type specific to Gaul before the Carolingian period.

At Jouarre, the crypts reflect the new monastic culture that emerged from the rule of Saint Columbanus. There are two rooms, one divided into nave and flanking aisles by columns crowned with sculpted capitals; these and the decorated sarcophagi found there, are revealing of the artistic culture of the Merovingian aristocracy of Gaul. The sarcophagus of Bishop Angilbert, set against the northern wall of the crypt and adorned with a bas-relief of the Last Judgment, is among the first examples of sculpture with monumental content. It contrasts with the low relief plant motifs carved on the other sarcophagi, which are said to be from Aquitaine.

Figured decoration for the Merovingian elite

Sculpted slab re-used as the cover of a sarcophagus in the *hypogeum* of Dunes, Poitiers. From left to right are found the Evangelists Matthew and John, symbolized by the angel and the eagle, at the sides of the archangels Raphael and Raguel. Below, an inscription mentions Lauritius, Varigatus, Hilary, and Martin. A further slab probably depicted the symbols of Luke and Mark, with the archangels Michael and Gabriel.

The highly decorated entrance to the funerary chapel

The stairs leading to the hypogeum of Dunes at Poitiers carry a sculpted decoration depicting, in order, four inter-twined strands ending in snake heads, fish, and a group of vegetation entwined with a braid. The sides of the entranceway doorposts are also decorated, with rosettes on the left and plant motifs on the right.

Remains of the abbey for women founded by Adon
Saint-Paul, Jouarre, Seine-et-Marne, interior view of the crypt, end of the seventh–beginning of the eighth century. The rectangular-plan edifice is divided into three main spaces by two rows of three columns with richly decorated Corinthian or composite marble capitals. It shelters seven sarcophagi, including that of Angilbert and the tomb of Abbess Theodechildis.

The evolution of sculpted motifs
Saint-Paul, Jouarre, Seine-et-Marne, cenotaph of Theodechildis, end of the seventh–beginning of the eighth century. An inscription in Latin verse on the two faces of the cenotaph pays homage to the virtues of the abbey's first abbess. The whole is decorated with a motif of scallops carved in perfectly classical style.

Variations in the tradition

Saint-Paul, Jouarre, Seine-et-Marne, capitals, end of the seventh–beginning of the eighth century. Re-use, classical models, and innovations in the treatment of capitals.

Above left: Classical model, composite type, decorated with fluting and crowned with a row of ovolos resting on a band of beads.

Above right: Corinthian type, with a set of large, intricate Byzantine acanthus leaves. In the space left free between the tendrils, the leaves appear carved flat, along with two anchors and two intertwined serpents. The columnar die of the abacus is decorated with engraved chevrons.

Below: Composite type, with four large, strongly curved acanthus leaves serving to support the highly disengaged handles above it; the scrolled ends of the handles are decorated with four-petaled flowers, like those carved on the abacus. This example perfectly illustrates the originality of Merovingian capitals.

The Monolith of the Mausoleum of Theodoric

Mausoleum of Theodoric
Detail of the dome of the mausoleum or rotunda of Theodoric, Ravenna, beginning of the sixth century. This monolithic dome is adorned with a curious ornamental band at the level of the cornice, an unusual element that gives a distinctive character to this funerary structure made from large blocks of stone.

The mausoleum is a funerary monument intended to house one or more tombs. In paleo-Christian architecture, the term designates a monumental tomb that has no liturgical furniture and which is called *hypogeum* when half-underground.

The mausoleum of Theodoric in Ravenna was built for the king of the Ostrogoths before his death in 526. This central-plan structure owes its architectural renown to the great monolith that serves as its domed roof. Crudely cut, it now has a long crack in its south side. It is around a meter thick, more than 10.9 m in diameter, and weighs an estimated 300 tons.

On the inside of the dome, a large central disk carries a Maltese cross painted in red and green and decorated with precious stones.

Outside, twelve heavy rectangular pierced lugs circle the dome; they are inscribed with the names of the eight Apostles and the four Evangelists. They are placed in the following order: + SCS PETRVS, SCS PAVLVS, SCS ANDREAS, SCS IACOBVS, SCS IOHANNES, SCS FELIPPVS, SCS MATTEVS, SCS MATHIAS, SCS MARCVS, SCS LVCAS, SCS THOMAS, SCS SIMEON. It has sometimes been suggested that

these inscriptions were made after construction of the mausoleum.

At the summit of the roofstone a disk projects 3.75 m above the monolith, at whose center can be seen a block 0.75 m long, 0.55 m wide, and 0.30 m high. Around this were cut six rectangular slots, clearly intended for an ornament quite unlike the cross found there today.

Theodoric's choice of a monolith may relate to tombs in his native land dating back to megalithic times, and in particular to the huge stones used to roof the funerary chambers of *tumuli*. At all events, this enormous stone is an assertion of power and strength, which alludes to the celestial firmament; the cross painted inside, probably reflects the sovereign's desire to place himself under the protection of the Christian divinity.

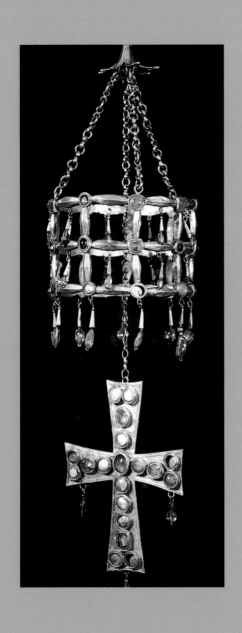

AT THE PERIPHERY

From Spain to the British Isles

Page 97
Discovery of a treasury of royal crowns
Crown from the treasury of Guarrazar, Toledo, mid-seventh century. This crown, made from a lattice of bent gold leaf studded with cabochon stones and a garland of amethyst beads, from which hangs a cross pattée, admirably demonstrates the dexterity of the Visigoths of Toledo in the field of goldsmith work. They buried this treasure when the Muslims from North Africa invaded Spain. (Museo del Prado, Madrid)

The metamorphosis of capitals
Capital showing Daniel in the lions' den, San Pedro de la Nave, Zamora, second half of the seventh century. From this point, capitals became the carriers of sacred history, with great scenes from the Holy Scripture placed under imposts carved with scrollwork, vines, birds, and masks. Daniel in the lions' den is depicted in very low relief in a space that leaves ample room for the development of decoration on a smooth surface.

With the spread of Christianity throughout the Roman Empire, the extreme west of the Roman Mediterranean was eventually converted. The arrival of the migrating Germanic peoples, especially the Visigoths, transformed the Iberian Peninsula into a dazzlingly creative kingdom. In the Guarrazar crowns, we recognize the finest examples of the art of goldsmithery and metalwork in which the Visigoths excelled, and which constitute their main artistic contribution to the West. In architecture, the Visigoths adopted the firmly implanted paleo-Christian basilican tradition, following Italian and North African models.

Traditionally, Visigothic art is known for toreutics (the art of making ornamental reliefs by embossing or chasing techniques) and goldsmithery. By the end of the fifth century, Visigothic treasures provided a visible expression of the great wealth that had been earned by the Visigothic elite through trade. The most spectacular objects, made of chased gold and decorated with cabochons and inlay, are the crowns donated to churches, where they were suspended above the altars; those of Rekeswinth (653–672) in the treasuries of Guarrazar and Swinthila, or that offered by Rekhared to Girona in honor of its martyr, Felix, all originated in royal workshops. In the area of personal jewelry, the fashion for small lyrate brooches replaced the older style of fibulas.

The Visigothic Iberian peninsula

In the sixth century, the Third Council of Toledo (589) and the conversion to Catholicism of Rekhared, the king of the Visigoths, gave a powerful impulse to the development of religious and monumental architecture, especially in the central area of the kingdom. Toledo, where Athanagild settled in 567, became the capital of the kingdom under Leowigild (572–586). Around this city evolved a court art whose influence spread to the borders of the kingdom.

The earliest contemporary references to the Christianization of the new Visigothic capital of Toledo date back to the seventh century. It is known that the Ninth (655) and Eleventh (675) Councils of Toledo took place in the church of Santa María. This may have then been the cathedral, but in the absence of information as to its location, we may assume that the council meetings were held in an urban church. The other Christian buildings mentioned in the available sources were all located outside the city walls. The most famous of these, the church of Santa Leocadia, better known today from excavations, hosted a total of four councils during the seventh century and several bishops were buried there. In Toledo, as in the majority of the major cities of Late Antiquity, there were several monasteries on the outskirts of the city; seventh-century accounts mention those of Santa Cruz and Santa Eulalia.

During the seventh century, an original architecture began to evolve on the Iberian Peninsula that can be compared with that of the Syrian or Byzantine monuments of the sixth century. The churches of San Pedro de la Nave, San Juan de Baños, founded in 661 near Palencia, and Santa María de Quintanilla de las Viñas, all small-

Crowns for the altar
Crown from the treasury of
Guarrazar, Toledo, c. 653–672.
A repoussé gold plaque is
studded with precious stones and
cabochons in the Byzantine style.
From it hang a cross and pendant
letters forming the name
Rekeswinth. This treasury, along
with that of Torredonjimeno
(Jaén), constitutes one of the
most important collections of
goldsmith work of the
European High Middle Ages.
(Museo Arqueológico Nacional,
Madrid)

Page 101 above
**The statement of the
tripartite chevet**
San Juan de Baños, Cerrato,
Palencia, plan, mid-seventh
century. Archaeological excavations have revealed that two
lateral extensions, resembling the
crossing of a low transept, were
originally present. Onto these
two rectangular chapels were
grafted, giving the chevet a
tripartite appearance. Side
porches completed the whole.

Page 101 below
**The oldest dated
Visigothic construction**
San Juan de Baños, Cerrato,
Palencia, exterior, mid-seventh
century. The compact volumes,
irregular stonework, and narrow
loopholes going onto wider
internal openings in the upper
part of the arcaded nave wall
attest to the age of this Visigothic
structure, which, despite reconstruction work has suffered no
addition with the exeption of the
bell-cote.

scale structures, present a very compartmented internal plan intended to facilitate vaulting of enclosed spaces. Theirs is some of the earliest vaulting on the peninsula. The basilical plan, usually with nave and flanking aisles, derives from paleo-Chris-tian architecture. The eastend is normally tripartite and right-angled. The con-struction uses large hewn blocks, the interior walls have simple engaged columns, and the window arches are not splayed.

Important fragments of Visigothic sculpture have survived from certain monu-mental buildings and episcopal complexes of the seventh century. The most active workshop was in Mérida, where pilasters sculpted on four sides, chancel plaques, and liturgical furniture equal in quality to contemporary Roman or Ravennate ex-

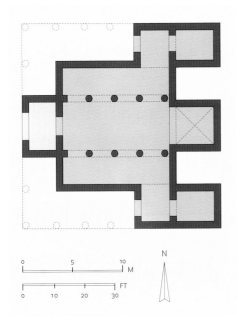

amples are preserved. In Mérida, the influence of Byzantine art can sometimes be perceived, as in Portugal (Lisbon) or at Saamasas, in the Lugo region. Beveled edges, low relief, and geometric motifs varied only rarely with plant or figurative carvings create a highly decorative style, a kind of "metalworking" on stone.

In Old Castile, the church of San Juan de Baños is attributed to Rekeswinth by an inscription placed above the triumphal arch, but the date that it gives (657) is wrong; the church dates from 652. It is a good example of a small-scale basilical plan with nave and flanking aisles. The latter are separated by horseshoe arcades resting on columns with Corinthian capitals and culminating in three rectangular apses, all freestanding. There are small apses on the arms of the transept. This rather unusual plan is also found in the later church of Santa Lucia del Trampal in Alcuesar. The western portico is entered through a horseshoe arch. The plan, with its internal divisions, the rectangular form of the apses, and the classical-style masonry is typical of Visigothic churches.

The Church of Santa María de Melque, near Toledo, cannot be dated as precisely as Santa Lucía. For a long time it was thought to be Mozarabic influence, but recent studies have suggested that it dates back to the Visigothic era. Built in large blocks of stone, the church forms a Greek cross (both arms of equal length) and possesses an apse, entered through a horseshoe arch, and two square absidioles. The nave is barrel-vaulted and there is a dome over the crossing. This arrangement, combined with the construction techniques, tends to confirm that the building is Visigothic in origin.

San Pedro de la Nave, in the Zamora region, is certainly the best-known edifice of the period. Built in the second half of the seventh century, it was moved near El

A rigorously coherent elevation
Longitudinal section of San Juan de Baños, Cerrato, Palencia. The placement of the different levels shows more clearly in this section, which does not show reconstruction work. Section by Von Pelt.

Visigothic sculptors favored geometric motifs
Detail of a frieze from San Juan de Baños, Cerrato, Palencia, mid-seventh century. The compan-drawn design is chamfered; the homogeneous composition consists of circles intersecting to form quatrefoils, and demonstrates the rigorously geometric nature of Visigothic sculpted ornamentation.

Campillo in the 1930s. It has a very harmonious plan. The nave is higher than the aisles. A kind of transept is prolonged on the exterior by a projecting porch at each of its two ends. The building affords graduated proportions unfolding from a cruciform plan. The chevet has a single rectangular apse. The large, well-hewn blocks of stone, and the presence of a room of unknown purpose above the apse, to which the sole access is via an opening in the upper part of the triumphal arch, are very characteristic of Visigothic religious structures.

A similar typology is found in Santa Comba de Bande (Orense) and San Pedro de la Mata (Toledo). In San Pedro de la Nave, the presence of painted friezes, sculpted bases, and capitals adorned in low relief show both the influence of classical forms and the search for novelty in the two workshops responsible for the decoration. The enduring predilection for Corinthian capitals, in particular, is noteworthy. The choir of the church features an iconographic program emphasizing Salvation. Episodes from the stories of Daniel and Isaac and the figures of apostles Peter, Paul, Philip, and Thomas are represented. The capitals and bases are decorated with birds and vines. Elsewhere, decorative friezes of lesser quality with geometric motifs run the length of the walls of the nave, the transept, and the chevet.

Santa María de Quintanilla de las Viñas, in the Burgos region, is probably the most recent Visigothic monument; it is dated to the end of the seventh or the beginning of the eighth century. This is confirmed in a document of 879, which refers to the church's restoration. In addition, an inscription on one of the capitals in the apse, and another on a external frieze show a monogram which in all likelihood iden-

Page 103
The internal space conveys the cohesion of the structure
San Juan de Baños, Cerrato, Palencia, interior, mid-seventh century. This edifice with nave and flanking aisles separated by horseshoe arches on columns and Corinthian capitals gives evidence of the spatial equilibrium of Visigothic churches. The direct lighting of the nave comes from the windows in the apses and from the main door.

tifies the patrons who endowed the foundation or restoration. Researchers are divided on the chronology of the sculpted decoration of Santa María, although the church itself is fully characteristic of the Visigothic period.

The basilica is not perfectly preserved; it originally presented a nave, partitioned spaces in the side-aisles, and a transept extended by a small rectangular room at the end of each arm, which gave it the aspect of a Latin cross. The nave was at one time preceded by a vestibule itself joined to two small, enclosed spaces. Of the chevet, only the projecting portion remains today; this is a rectangular apse which gives onto the crossing. The transept has lost its two extensions. The highly compartmentalized interior space is lighted by high, very narrow windows. The basilica was constructed with large blocks of stone and is decorated along its entire circumference with friezes sculpted with geometric and foliage motifs in shallow basrelief. In the chevet, monograms framed by medallions follow a Byzantine model. The various interlacing ornamentations and decorative motifs have their roots in late classical art, Sassanid art, and Eastern textiles. Its kinship with contemporary Visigothic gold work is clear.

The interior decoration of Santa María de Quintanilla de las Viñas is famous for bas-reliefs so shallow as almost to seem engraved. They present narrative themes and are notable for the expressionism of the figures. On either side of the triumphal arch, they show Christ Blessing, two flying angels, and, at the entry to the apse, winged figures supporting a *clipeus* (round shield) containing personifications of the sun on one side and of the moon on the other. This complex iconography is stylistically related to Late Antiquity while at the same time looking forward to Romanesque art.

São Gião de Nazaré in Portugal, not far from Lamego, offers a very compartmentalized structure and a plan similar to that of Santa María de Quintanilla; the transepts are shorter than the nave, and the crossing gives directly onto the apse.

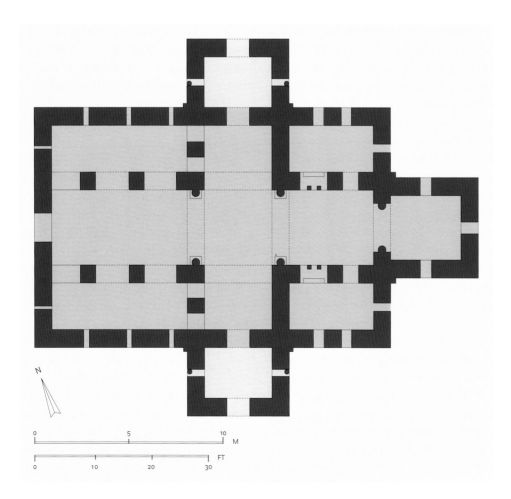

A cruciform plan grafted onto a basilica
San Pedro de la Nave, Zamora, plan, second half of the seventh century. The cruciform structure using the Latin cross overlays the plan of a rectangular basilica. The extension of the western arm of the cross defines the nave, which is flanked by aisles.

N

0   5   10 M

0   10   20   30 FT

Vigorous exterior volumes combined with small dimensions
San Pedro de la Nave, Zamora, exterior, second half of the seventh century. The construction of a dam threatened this edifice, which was rebuilt at the edge of the village of El Campillo, where it displays its elegant mass in which the balanced volume of the nave and aisles is juxtaposed with the height of the transept arms.

Large blocks of stone with sharp seams
Detail of a gemel window of San Pedro de la Nave, Zamora, second half of the seventh century. This window presents a fine example of the prefabrication of architectural elements inserted in the masonry. It also breaks with the Roman use of rubble set in cement and the alternation of courses of brick and stone in Byzantine construction.

A highly decorative religious message

Capital showing the Sacrifice of Isaac, San Pedro de la Nave, Zamora, second half of the seventh century. Abraham, grasping his son Isaac by the hair, prepares to sacrifice him. The Divine hand then appears and points out the ram in the thicket, which will take the place of Isaac. The appearance of the historiated storied capital arose from a desire to teach and a concern to place the iconographic accent on either side of the main square space of the edifice.

Below
Symbol preferred to image

San Pedro de la Nave, Zamora, second half of the seventh century. Detail of the sculpted friezes found in the apse, choir, and on the east wall of the transept, on the capitals of the entrance and the frames of the windows in the apse. It combines "braided" circles with Maltese crosses, wheels or rosettes, chancel arches and highly stylized vines.

Page 106
Historiated capitals at the crossing

San Pedro de la Nave, Zamora, interior, second half of the seventh century. The junction of the transept and the nave forms a cross, framed by four large identical horseshoe arches resting on columns. The bases and capitals of the columns display remarkable sculpted decoration, which gives the appearance of being carved directly into the wall.

Visigothic or Mozarabic architecture

Santa María de Melque, Toledo, exterior. The edifice has a Greek cross plan, extended by a rectangular apse and a porch pierced with three openings. Its massive appearance, due to its irregular masonry of enormous blocks of granite, laid without mortar, to façades with few windows or openings, and to the layering of its volumes, is softened by the rounded treatment of the corners.

The partitioned spaces in Visigothic tradition
Santa María de Melque, Toledo, interior. The interior space of the edifice is entirely vaulted and is characterized by a partitioning of space effected by horseshoe arches.

The nave is independent of the side-aisles, which are themselves compartmentalized. By contrast, central-plan buildings at Valdecevadar, Olivenza in the Badajoz region, the mausoleum of São Frutuoso in Montelios (begun at the end of the seventh century), Santa Comba de Bande in Galicia (Orense), and San Pedro de la Mata gave priority to a plan and elevation derived from a Greek cross. The central space communicates with these arms by means of double (Olivenza) or triple arches (Montelios) supported by columns. With São Pedro de Balsemão in Portugal, these cruciform buildings constitute a group apart.

The religious architecture of the Visigothic period is characterized by compartmentalized interiors, the play of proportions, and elegant stonework. In the more lavish examples, the unity of the stonework is broken by sculpted string courses on the outside and figurative decorations inside. In ornament of this kind, the highly

Above

In the image of the Tomb of Galla Placidia in Ravenna
São Frutuoso de Montelios, near Braga, Portugal, exterior, dated 665. The edifice displays a cruciform plan with a crossing capped by a small tower. Its outer covering presents, in low projection, an alternation of semicircular and triangular arches, finished with a thin ornamental band that serves to lighten the monolithic presentation of the walls.

Below

The spread of the horseshoe arch
São Frutuoso de Montelios, near Braga, Portugal, interior, dated 665. Three of the arms of the cross are treated as horseshoe-shaped apses hollowed out of the solid masonry forming the square outside walls. Behind the two central arcades of diminishing size, small complex shapes are generated, they are covered by vaults resting on colonettes. There are four such spaces in the arms of the cross an six in the apse.

restrictive frame, extremely shallow relief, exaggerated proportions of the person-
ages, simultaneously frontal and profile representation of the body and the styliza-
tion of the eyes, hands, and nose are the principal stylistic traits. These works show
a family resemblance to many contemporary works, such as the sculpted reliefs of
Italy and even illuminated Irish manuscripts.

Thick walls and vaults
Santa Comba de Bande, Orense,
interior, seventh century. The
modest dimensions of the church
and the thickness of its walls made
it possible to use brick vaulting
throughout the church. The arms
of the cross feature barrel vaults.

Page 113 above
**Organization of volumes
around a vaulted crossing**
Santa Comba de Bande, Orense,
view of the vault of the crossing,
seventh century. The transept
crossing is ornamented by means
of a convex groined vault built in
a low tower whose walls rest on
four massive horseshoe arches.

Page 113 below
**Annexes (now used as sacristies)
surround the sanctuary**
Santa Comba de Bande, Orense,
exterior, seventh century. The
structure, composed of irregular
blocks of stone, includes a rectangular apse, a square tower with
window openings, and a bell-cote
of later construction preceded by
a small porch open on three sides
and originally endowed with two
side additions. Excavations also
revealed the existence of square-
plan extensions to the west and
east arms of the cross.

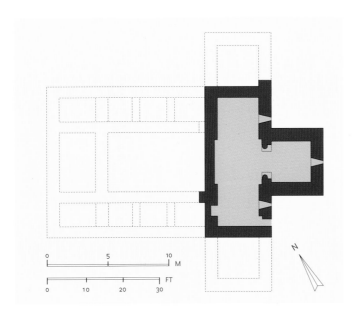

Original Greek plan-cross
Quintanilla de las Viñas, Lara, plan, second half of the seventh century. The edifice currently standing has been reduced to an open transept and a square apse. Excavations have revealed a nave and aisles, as well as a porch endowed with two lateral extensions.

Friezes that evoke metalwork
Details of the sculpted bands of decoration of Quintanilla de las Viñas, Lara, second half of the seventh century. These decorative bands display medallions tracing stylized scrolls that enclose leaves, vines, and birds. The variety and oriental nature of the motifs of Visigothic sculpture are clearly in evidence.

Very low relief and extreme schematization of the human figure

Bas-relief of an impost supporting the entrance arch in the apse of Quintanilla de las Viñas, Lara, second half of the seventh century. Two flying angels face each other; they hold a circular medallion inset with the head of the radiating sun. Their silhouettes, marked by incised lines, stand out against a flat ground.

A sculpted decoration that breaks with the naturalistic formulas of Antiquity

Decoration on the theme of the glorification of Christ, Quintanilla de las Viñas, Lara, second half of the seventh century. Two angels flank Christ, whose majesty is emphasized here by a corded double halo. The latter holds a cross pattée, as does the angel on the right. Not a trace of corporeal reality appears in the play of lines of the robes, of the angels' wings, or in the repetitive schematized faces.

**Sculptured friezes
encircle the edifice**
Quintanilla de las Viñas, Lara, view
of the chevet, second half of the
seventh century. The chevet is
notable for the three projecting
blocks and the three extensive
sculptured friezes. The two lower
friezes extend around the entire
eastern side of the transept's
arms. Architecture thus becomes
an integral part of a rich
decorative repertory.

Page 118

**Massive towers mark
the edifices of the British Isles**
Monkwearmouth in County
Durham, Great Britain, exterior,
last quarter of the seventh
century. The most original
elements of Anglo-Saxon architecture remain the beautiful
towers that are often placed
between the sanctuary and the
nave. The majority are rectangular. The Gothic nave is a later
addition.

**The emergence of a monumental
sculpture**
Monkwearmouth in County
Durham, Great Britain, view of the
porch, last quarter of the seventh
century. The earliest sculpted
elements are usually architectural
fragments. Those from the
porch of Monkwearmouth
number among the oldest.

The Isolation of the British Isles

The arrival of Christians during the fifth century, Augustine's mission to England in
597, and the marriage of Aethelbert, king of Kent, to a Frankish Christian princess,
are significant landmarks in the Christianization of the British Isles. To these might
be added the conversion of the king of Essex and his choice of London as capital,
and the Christianization of Northumbria and East Anglia. By the middle of the seventh century, the majority of the islands' kingdoms were Christianized. This period
saw the flowering of an independent art derived from the tradition of Late Antiquity and the heritage of Frankish and nature influences.

The isolation of the British Isles fostered the originality of their art, which was
enriched by exchanges between monasteries. Sources such as the Venerable Bede
tell us that the king of Northumbria sent his daughters to the abbey of Jouarre to
complete their education, and that one of the characteristics of the Anglo-Saxon
kingdoms was an impressively strong teaching tradition in the cultural and ecclesi-

astical domains. Contacts with northern European countries were clearly, constant and intense, as is shown by recurrent decorative themes such as tracery. The precious objects discovered in the seventh-century tombs like that of Sutton Hoo offer evidence of workshops specializing in personal ornaments in gold and other precious metals for the use of high-ranking patrons. Jewels, arms, and utilitarian objects in gold inlaid with other materials frequently carry decorations in cloisonné enamel, generally in the characteristic blues and reds of Anglo-Saxon art. The presence in the islands' funerary treasures of plates and dishes, Byzantine liturgical objects worked in gold, and coins from Merovingian Gaul tell us much about trade with the continent or the eastern Mediterranean.

Unfortunately, no architecture from this period is existent, and we therefore know little about it. However, the opulence of certain tombs, such as that of Saint Cuthbert († 687) – his richly sculpted wooden reliquary casket can be seen today in the treasury of Durham Cathedral – indicates the spectacular artistic flowering that spread from the monasteries and cathedrals during the seventh century. Sculpted

The sobriety of monumental tradition
Monkwearmouth in County Durham, Great Britain, interior, last quarter of the seventh century. Unity, monumental severity, and vertical symmetry characterize the appearance of the walls in the earliest Christian architecture in Great Britain.

Left

British sculpted crosses

Detail of the shaft of the cross of Bewcastle, late seventh century. During the age of barbarian invasions, the British Isles experienced an isolation that encouraged the originality of its art. The sculpted bas-reliefs illustrating the Nativity, the Crucifixion, the Resurrection, and the Ascension afford fine examples. This representation of Christ was intended to inspire meditation, as were the sculpted crosses erected outside churches.

Right

The predominance of interlace patterns

A side view of the cross of Bewcastle, dating from the late seventh century, illustrates a typical decoration of interlace patterns. Bas-reliefs are ornamented with meandering plant motifs and floral scrolls.

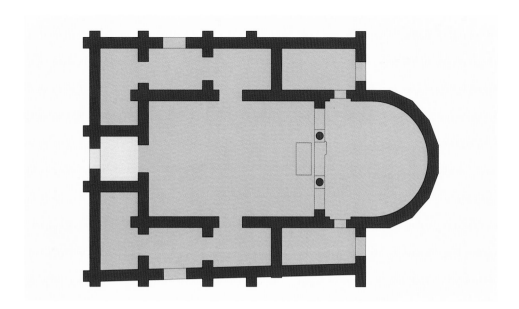

The use of partitioned spaces
Saint Mary of Reculver, Kent, plan, seventh century. This church with apse is organized around a system of compartments: a triple arcade in a partition wall connected the apse to the nave and two doors at the ends of the nave gave access to two rooms serving as porches.

elements from the doors of Monkwearmouth in the region of Durham, dated to the last quarter of the century, also survive.

The oldest Anglo-Saxon architecture is known mostly from archaeological excavations, which have revealed the existence of a considerable number of simple structures widely dispersed through the land. The most popular plan presents a rectangular nave without side-aisles, sometimes flanked by partitioned spaces known as a *porticus*. Apses are rare, and crypts the exception. One exception to this rule was Saint Mary's at Reculver in Kent. This seventh-century monastic church possessed a rectangular nave extending into an apse semicircular on the inside and polygonal on the outside. Communication between nave and chancel was generally by a triple arcade. All Saints church at Brixworth (Northamptonshire) is typical of the layout of the seventh-century church, but its scale is that of an important monument. Even though it probably dates to the eighth century, it clearly illustrates the interior partitioning that is an essential trait of the earliest Anglo-Saxon churches.

Among the surviving examples of monumental sculpture in stone are the crosses of Northumbria and Ireland. Those of Bewcastle and Ruthwell may date back to the seventh century, although their narrative scenes and superlative repertory of tracery and geometric motifs might equally point to a later date. Illustrated Italian manuscripts brought to the British Isles undoubtly influenced the local style, which combined classical reminiscences with native tastes. It led to the production of highly stylized illuminations, particularly in Ireland; we may cite the *Book of Durrow* (about 680) and, in the eighth century, the *Book of Kells* which constituted a culminating point in the insular tradition and had considerable influence on the earliest Carolingian illumination.

Scandinavian architecture of the fifth and the seventh centuries is little known. We can get some idea of its richness from surviving objects from the same period, ornamented with tracery and representations derived from the art of the Siberian and Scythian steppes. The Vikings traded with southern Europe and imported Mediterranean objects, thus transmitting the classical tradition to the northernmost regions.

Manuscripts of the isles
Manuscript of the Irish Evangelistary in St. Gall, after 750. The development of monasteries and Christian communities called for the reproduction of Bibles and religious books. Schools of scribes produced magnificent manuscripts, employing vivid colors and a variety of motifs, prominently featuring interlace patterns, spirals, animals, and the symbols of the Evangelists. This manuscript demonstrates the technical prowess of the Anglo-Saxon workshops of illuminators. (Library of the abbey, St. Gall, Cod. Sang. 51, p. 266)

THE CAROLINGIAN WORLD

Palaces and Cathedrals

The Arabs who dominated Spain, Septimania, and part of southern France were halted in their northward advance by the soldiers of Charles Martel at the battle of Poitiers, on 17 October 732. The dynasty of the Pepinids became dominant when in 751 Pépin the Short, backed by the Pope, was crowned king in Soissons. Succeeding the Merovingian dynasty and Childerich III, the Carolingians reigned until 987, when they were replaced by the Capetians.

Charlemagne ruled a vast territory bounded by the Ebro and the Elbe. By having himself crowned emperor in Rome by Pope Leo III, he restored the empire. Charlemagne and his successors restored or created many prestigious political and cultural institutions. Their power was legitimized by the ritual that granted religious sanction to the head of state. Despite this universalist effort, the unity of the empire did not last long: following Frankish tradition the empire was divided among the king's sons. Charlemagne had only one successor, Louis the Pious, but in 817 the next generation saw its territories divided between the sons of Louis' first wife – Lothair, the eldest, Pépin (Aquitaine), and Louis (Bavaria) and Charles, son of Judith of Bavaria, his second wife. After the death of Louis and his second son, Pépin, the empire was divided again, in 843, by the Treaty of Verdun. Lothair, the new emperor, reigned over Lotharingia, which brought together the territories from Frisia to Italy and Provence; Louis, called the German, inherited eastern France or Germany; to Charles the Bald fell the western part of France.

In addition to the rivalries between brothers that had weakened the empire since 826 and which persisted among the descendants of Lothair († 855), the security of the frontier was often threatened: the Arabs invaded from the south, the Scandinavians from the north, and the Hungarians from the east. After 840, these dangers intensified. In each new kingdom, the nobility strengthened its power at the expense of the monarch's. The ecclesiastical hierarchy, too, sought to enhance its authority after the death of Charles (877) by imposing conditions at the crowning of his successor, Louis the Stammerer. But it was the nobility that thereafter decided the royal succession, rejecting Charles III in favor of a son of Robert the Strong, Odo, comte de Paris and duc des Francs. In the space of a hundred years, Carolingians and Robertians were elected in turn by the now all-powerful nobility. Not until 935 were three Carolingians elected successively; another Robertian, Hugues the Great, called Capet, finally gained power in 987.

The marquis gradually established themselves as potentates in their own right. A series of events precipitated this. Odo, the most powerful of the marquis, was elected king. Boso, the brother-in-law of Charles the Bald, was proclaimed king of the Provence in 879. And the Marquis de Gothie rejected Louis the Stammerer's authority over his territories in the Narbonne area. The marquis now had a role as "marcher lords". Throughout the land, from Flanders to Brittany, western Burgundy, and Catalonia, principalities, duchies, and counties flourished in the wake of internal struggles and became increasingly independent of the royal administration. The principalities illustrate this process; by their annexation of

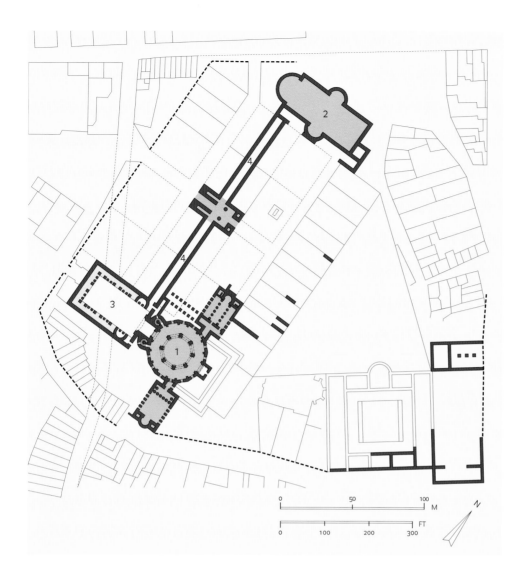

The palace, center of power
Palace of Charlemagne, Aachen, plan, 790–805. The central space is flanked on the north by the royal room and on the south by the Palatine Chapel. Among Charlemagne's residences, this architectural realization was the most remarkable.
1 Palatine chapel
2 *Aula palatine*
3 *Atrium*
4 Gallery

ecclesiastical powers and local administration and by the independence of their economies – they struck coins bearing the image of the ruling prince – they demonstrated that only their duty as vassals any longer connected them to the monarchy.

Thus, during the Carolingian period, when the architecture of the Early Middle Ages attained its definitive form, paving the way for the long creative flowering of the Middle Ages, the practice of architecture in many ways reflected the political circumstances we have described. The early part of the period and the reigns of Charlemagne (766/800–814) and Louis the Pious (814–840) were marked by the imposition of a unified style giving monumental expression to the unitary, centralizing power; as the regional powers asserted themselves, this aspiration toward stylistic unity crumbled away.

Palatine Architecture

The Carolingian period was one of intense architectural activity. The structures that it produced were based on models from Late Antiquity. Many surviving monuments in Germany, Switzerland, Belgium, and France still illustrate the vitality of the Carolingian monarchs' architectural policy of splendor and grandeur. More than 400 monasteries, twenty-seven new cathedrals, and about a hundred royal residences were built during the reigns of Charlemagne and Louis the Pious, in an empire that encompassed most of western Europe. They bear striking witness to the architectural drive of the Carolingian sovereigns.

Charlemagne established his main palace at Herstal, although from early in his reign he moved from one residence to another. But soon his need to compete with

Page 129
Homage to the work of Justinian (527–565)
Palatine Chapel of Charlemagne, Aachen, interior, 790–805. The polygonal structure with a two-story elevation, on the model of San Vitale, Ravenna (sixth century), gave rise to a type of church highly esteemed by court circles throughout the Middle Ages.

Eastern potentates and earlier rulers of the Roman Empire led him to construct a new and sumptuous residence, which could house not only his court but his chapel, treasury, and library. He decided to locate it at Aachen.

Palace architecture had to adapt to these new needs. In the palace, the imperial administration gave rise to a certain number of domestic and political duties to be carried out by those who organized and oversaw the court of the ruler. The palatine count was responsible for the administration of justice, the chancellor was responsible for accounts and the chamberlain, or steward, kept watch over the treasury and the king's guard. The high constable commanded the marshals and supervised not only the stables but all travel and transport – matters of primary importance for a partly itinerant government. Finally, it was necessary to accommodate stores of food and appoint those responsible for its provision; the space allotted to wine, for example, was organized by the cupbearer.

Charlemagne entrusted the construction of his palace at Aachen to Odo of Metz in 790. It was a vast complex, at once private residence, ceremonial hall, place of worship, military headquarters, and the state's administrative, judicial, and cultural

A perfect imitation of classical capitals
Detail of the gallery arcades of the upper store, Palatine Chapel of Charlemagne, Aachen, 790–805. The large arches located above the arcades of the ground floor and below the drum of the dome are divided by two rows of tiered columns with capitals carved in white marble. Most of these are re-used Roman or Byzantine works. The capitals carved specially for this monument demonstrate the expertise of the Carolingian sculptors, who were able to reproduce classical models with precision.

The decorative use of materials
The arcades of the ground floor of the Palatine Chapel of Charlemagne, Aachen, rest on massive pillars faced with porphyry and polychrome marbles, creating a dazzling decorative effect.

center. The whole was organized in a well-ordered plan with the palace in the center. The square palace was bordered on the south by the Palatine Chapel and on the north by the *Aula* on the site of what is today the city hall. This symbolic ensemble, the seat of authority of the all-powerful emperor, was partially completed in 805. On Epiphany of that year, Pope Leo III consecrated the Palatine Chapel.

The chapel at Aachen palace seems to have been directly inspired by that of San Vitale in Ravenna, built under Justinian in the sixth century. Fronted by a rectangular courtyard reminiscent of the *atria* of Roman basilicas, the chapel is of central plan; the exterior is a sixteen-sided polygon while, inside, an annular ambulatory surmounted by high galleries gives onto the central rotunda, which is crowned with a dome. A rectangular arm extended to the east, while to the west, a tower-porch flanked by two stairways permitting access to the galleries dominated the entrance. The faithful could gather in the lower part, while the upper floor was

**An accomplished
architectural structure**
The dome of the Palatine Chapel
of Charlemagne, Aachen, rising
from a drum pierced with windows
supported on octagonal arcades,
has been given a decoration
imitating the original mosaic; it
represents Christ on His throne
acclaimed by the twenty-four
elders of the Apocalypse.
Courtiers could contemplate this
scene from the gallery.

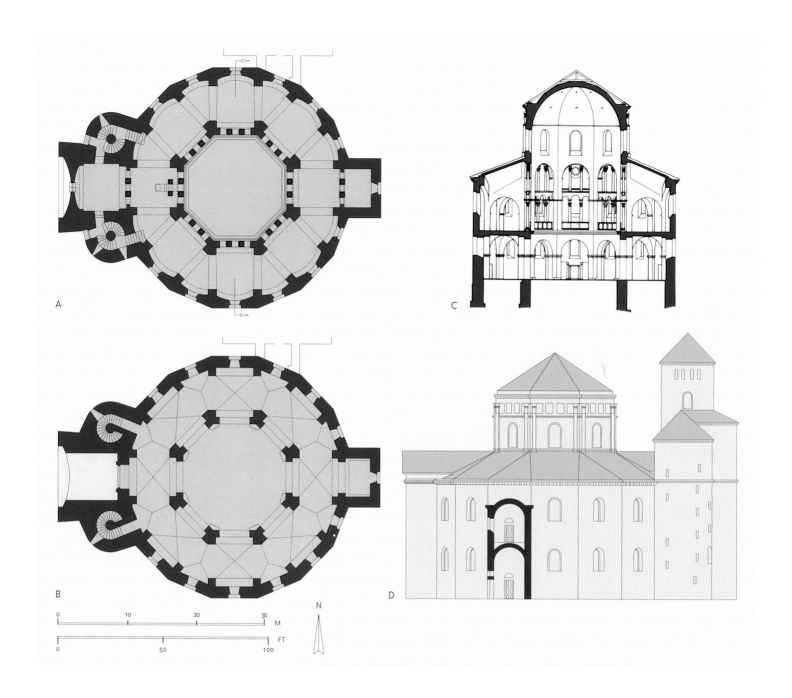

reserved for royalty. The ambulatory is groin-vaulted and opens on the center through eight round arches. The elevation of the central space comprises two levels: the large arcades and a storey of galleries. Above this rises the drum of the dome, pierced with windows.

One notable characteristic of the chapel at Aachen is the adaptation of the architecture to the way in which it was used. The courtiers took their seats in the gallery around Charlemagne's throne, which was placed opposite the choir, behind a grill that opened for important ceremonies. From there could be seen the small rectangular apse, which has been replaced by a Gothic choir. This small eastern sanctuary set off the majestic proportions of the polygon, whose visual impact was further enhanced by the westwork and the *atrium*. The apse had two levels, each dedicated to cults particularly emphasized during Carolingian period: that of Mary, in the lower part, and of the Savior, in the upper.

In the Carolingian period, the Palatine Chapel in Aachen was richly decorated. The altar frontal was worked in gold, the bronze balustrades of the galleries were ornamented with an acanthus-leaf pattern, and the mosaics that adorned the dome completely dominated the interior space. This decoration is known through

An influential architectural model
Plan and cross sections of the Palatine Chapel of Charlemagne, Aachen, 790–805. An octagonal central core is surrounded by a two-story envelope. The whole is extended at the east by a rectangular sanctuary. At the west, the façade presents a westwork flanked by two stairway towers.

A Plan of the upper story (barrel-vaulted)

B Plan of the ground floor (groin-vaulted)

C Cross section

D Northern façade

The Ravenna model

San Vitale, Ravenna, sixth century, inspired the Palatine Chapel of Aachen. The central room of the edifice is surrounded by tiers of arcades, which are divided by pairs of columns connected by arches. The very deep choir, extended by a polygonal apse, determines the principal axis of the edifice.

The last Ravenna-style sanctuary with a central plan

San Vitale, Ravenna, plan and cross section, sixth century. Octagonal plan with a narthex flanked by two stairway towers and preceded by an *atrium*. The central room, also octagonal, is separated from the ambulatory by semicircular exedrae,which enliven the internal elevation.

1 Narthex
2 Passages flanked by two round towers
3 Ambulatory
4 Octagonal central space
5 Chevet flanked by two absidioles with extensions

Bronze work during the Carolingian period
Decoration of the bronze door of the antechurch, Palatine Chapel of Charlemagne, Aachen, c. 800. This double swing door originally closed the porch of the westwork. It is a major work of the High Middle Ages, both for its dimensions – height: 4 m; depth: 4.2–5.9 cm; weight: 4 500 kg – and its decoration, composed of two lion heads. It is one of the few surviving bronze works of the Carolingian period.

Page 136
A masterful layering of architectural volumes
The choir of San Vitale, Ravenna, sixth century, reveals a deep apse framed by two absidioles that open onto two rectangular extensions flanked by secondary chapels.

descriptions and a drawing published in the eighteenth century. These describe the principal theme of the whole: the twenty-four Elders of the Apocalypse acclaiming the Divine Majesty enthroned.

This courtly art emerged from the center for literary studies that Charlemagne set up in the palace, and which attracted such famous scholars as Alcuin. The workshops of the court produced illuminated books which proved highly effective in the transmission of culture. The late eighth century Evangelistary of Godescalc reveals the growing importance of Italian and Byzantine models in the artistic circles of Charlemagne's court.

The prestige of the emperor and his palatine church at Aachen accounts for the influence exercised by the plan and even the elevation of this structure throughout the Middle Ages. It inspired a number of central plans, such as that of the Dalmatian church of Saint Donat in Zadar, or for the later church of Ottmarsheim in Alsace about 1030. Built for a member of the imperial court, the little oratory of Germigny-des-Prés (restored in the nineteenth century), in the Loire Valley, took the prestigious monument of Aachen as its symbolic model. The oratory was built by Theodulf, bishop of Orléans and abbot of Saint-Benoît-sur-Loire from 799 to 818, in the Gallo-Roman villa in Germaniacus, today Germigny-des-Prés. Today, it stands as one of the best and most informative examples of the palatine architecture of the Early Middle Ages. The Goth Theodulf was among the most famous men of letters of Charlemagne's court. He commissioned the designs for the rehabilitation of the existing villa and the construction of an oratory.

The *Catalogue des abbés de Fleury,* written at the end of the ninth century or the beginning of the tenth, describes the construction of the oratory in great detail and emphasizes the role played by Theodulf. It also indicates the prestige attached to this type of construction and affords a better understanding of Theodulf's intentions: "Not content to have the whole of this basilica rest on large arcades, he embellished the interior with a floral decoration in stucco as well as mosaics and endowed it with a floor in marble blocks, so that viewers never tired of gazing at it. In addition, at the base of the bell-tower, he had these verses placed in silver-colored letters: 'This temple, I, Theodulf, have consecrated in honor of God; you who enter here, whoever you may be, I beseech you, spare me a thought.'"

Aachen, the *Catalogue* states, was Theodulf's inspiration and model: "He [Theodulf] vied in this with Charlemagne, who, at that time, had built at his palace of Aachen a church of such splendor that its like could not be found in all of Gaul [...].

Evidence of Charlemagne's classicism
Detail of a railing from the galleries of the Palatine Chapel of Charlemagne, Aachen, 790–805. These cast and engraved bronze railings, originally gilded, are in four different models and thus provide insight into the evolution of the foundry workshop of Aachen. The oldest, showing frameworks that seem cut to shape rather than forged, present a decoration of geometric motifs. The most recent are in classical style, and are framed with pilasters with engraved capitals.

Theodulf consecrated his oratory to God, Creator and Preserver of All Things, and had a master artist represent, above the altar, cherubs covering the mercy seat of Divine Glory with their wings [...]." The mosaics of Germigny-des-Prés, despite a succession of damaging restorations, illustrate not only the use of this technique in late eighth-century Gaul but also the culture of the elite Carolingians.

Despite the *Catalogue,* the architecture of Aachen is alone in its use of a central plan. At Germigny-des-Prés, this is square; its four rectangular bays, forming a Greek cross, are barrel vaulted and supported by a central lantern, which has since been rebuilt as a dome. It originally comprised three well-lit storeys. During the Early Middle Ages, an apse opened on each of the four sides, completed to the east by two lateral absidioles. As in many contemporary monuments, polychrome stucco played an essential role in the chruch decoration. Theodulf's chapel perfectly defines the model of the small Carolingian palatine chapel in the very early ninth century, exemplifying the contemporary predilection for mosaic and stucco church ornament.

Study of the princely palaces and residences of the Carolingian period has made great strides in recent decades, mostly thanks to archaeology. The most common formula for a prince's palace was a rectangular plan of several, usually two storeys; one such palace or residence has been excavated at Doué-la-Fontaine, near Saumur. Its oldest stages of construction date back to the period of Louis the Pious, and it thus allows us to trace the evolution of palace architecture in the pre-Romanesque and Romanesque eras.

The Central Influence

Close to the center of Carolingian power, in the territory that is today Belgium, new architectural formulas coupled local traditions from Late Antiquity with the models in vogue at the court. The great Merovingian and Carolingian monastic centers often possessed several churches; two at Malonne or Saint-Amand; three at Nivelles, Corbie, Saint-Bertin, and Lobbes. The monastery of Malonne, known through the *Vie de Bertuin,* developed from the *cellula* of the saint, a *habitaculum* endowed with an oratory, and from the "parish" church *(ecclesia)*; there the saint preached to the faithful.

The monastic architecture of this region can be understood through the archae-

Page 139
The continuity of the imperial seat
This throne made of marble, styled as a replica of Solomon's throne, faced the choir in the gallery of the Palatine Chapel of Charlemagne, Aachen. There the emperor sat, surrounded by his courtiers. This arrangement originated in the Late Roman Empire and was revived in the Middle Ages for use in two-storey chapels.

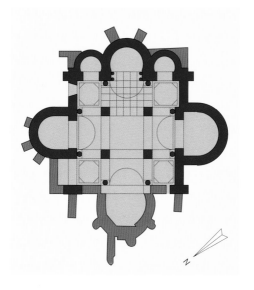

ological excavations carried out beneath the church of Sainte-Gertrude in Nivelles. This great monastic center was founded by Gertrude, who was interred there in 653 or 659. In the second half of the seventh century, it was a double abbey (for men and women). The main church, consecrated to Our Lady, was of basilical plan, with nave and flanking aisles and a semicircular apse. The monks' church, Saint-Paul, had a rectangular plan with rectangular apse. And Saint-Pierre was a funerary chapel. The last-named (today Sainte-Gertrude) was of rectangular plan; in an early restoration, it was given a rectangular apse in order to accommodate a tomb at its center. At the end of the ninth century, it adopted the basilical plan with nave and flanking aisles. An ambulatory was then built to direct the movement of pilgrims around the tomb, which was now surmounted by an altar. This eastern part of the edifice, which recalls the *Confessiones* of Rome, was extended to the west in the following century. At this point a westwork in Carolingian style was added, foreshadowing the great churches of the Romanesque era. Similar modifications took place at the abbey of Echternach, in Luxembourg, where Saint Willibrord is interred.

In Belgium, as elsewhere, great Carolingian architecture has too often disappeared, to be replaced by later structures which nevertheless retain the traces of Carolingian influence, such as the imposing westwork that joined the two towers and housed a counter-choir. The nave with alternating pillars of Saint-Ursmer in

Lantern tower used as a belfry
Germigny-des-Prés, interior view of the tower, 806. This originally had three storeys, formed successively by a triple arcade, a window outlined by an arch in stucco, and gemel windows. The third storey was removed in the nineteenth century.

Fidelity to classical tradition
Germigny-des-Prés interior view toward the east apse, 806. Very short freestanding colonnettes, with high pilaster bases, support the entrance arches of the apses. Another borrowing from the architecture of Late Antiquity is the dome on pendentives of the eastern apse.

Lobbes is a good example of the late use of Carolingian formulas and illustrates a technical apparatus all too rarely preserved.

The abbey of Lobbes was founded during the Merovingian period. Its principal church was built and consecrated (697) under Ursmer's tenure as abbot. In the mid-ninth century, the abbey housed a large community of seventy-eight monks. Of its three churches, only the abbey church remains, and the lack of documentary evidence means that we cannot date successive modifications. The nave, lit by a row of large windows set below the wooden ceiling, was originally separated from the aisles by large arcades resting on square pillars, divided into two smaller arcades by a column. A low transept precedes the flat east-end, which is raised above a crypt and flanked by two rectangular rooms. From the western side, the nave with three bays gives onto a sort of low transept, which makes up the fourth bay, flanked by two small chapels. The porch, surmounted by a gallery, is flanked in its turn

**The image of Christ evoked
by a symbolic figuration**
Mosaic of the eastern apse of
Germigny-des-Prés. The Ark of
the Covenant, framed by two
cherubim, appears under the
Divine hand that the two angels
worship. This decoration, part of
a group extended to the entire
church, is one of the few elements
spared in the drastic nineteenth-
century rebuilding.

by two towers. This antechurch reverts to the type used at Celles or Hastières, for example.

The alternating supports, the westwork, and the east-end raised above a crypt, are all characteristic elements of Carolingian architecture. Another characteristic was to extend the eastern part of the church behind the chevet, often in the form of external crypts. In this area, close to the center of power, the penchant for central-plan structures imitating the Palatine Chapel of Aachen was particularly wide-spread: Saint-Jean in Liège, Brugge, Muizen, and later, Saint-Pierre le Louvain and Torhout. Of this last site, archaeological excavations have revealed only a square plan in the form of a Greek cross; the elevation may have been of a form similar to that of the Germigny-des-Prés oratory.

Cathedrals and Monasteries

A great deal of construction took place in urban areas during the Carolingian period. The significant religious topography of the city of Metz is explained by the fact that Charlemagne had long lived in this city before he moved to Aachen. Under the bish-opric of Chrodegang (742–776), the episcopal complex comprised several build-ings, including the Cathedral of Saint-Étienne and the church of Sainte-Marie.

It was thus under Chrodegang that Saint-Étienne, the principal church of the complex, was redesigned. The old fifth-century church, enlarged in the sixth cen-tury, was preceded by an *atrium* and opened to the west, according to original sources, by means of a *turris* (tower), which would seem to indicate the presence of a westwork, or at least a tower-porch; its first floor housed a chapel dedicated to Saint Michael. To the east, the chevet gave directly onto a long, projecting transept; the choir was raised above the still partially conserved crypt. It was flanked by two stairway towers, and, further on, by two small lateral apses. Under Chrodegang, the church was further enhanced by new choir furnishings (a baldachin, a chancel or enclosure, and an episcopal throne).

On the other side of Saint-Étienne's *atrium* stands a church consecrated to the Virgin Mary, which is thought to date back to the seventh century. The original appearance of the center-plan Notre-Dame-la-Ronde is unknown to us, as the church was reconstructed during the Gothic period. The third structure restored by Chrodegang was the church of Saint-Pierre, founded in the seventh century by the bishop Goëric (629–641), in which he built a new choir with new furnishings: an ambo decorated with precious metals and a bishop's throne.

Chapels and conventual buildings (dormitories, refectories, kitchens) opened onto the canon's cloister, which stood to the south of the Cathedral of Saint-Étienne. The texts also mention an *episcopium,* or bishop's residence. In addition, at the southeast angle of the cloister stood Saint-Pierre-le-Vieux, which was probably built before the sixth century. This layout underscores the central role of the clois-ter, whose arcades connected the various structures. In the mid-eighth century, a small building dedicated to Saint Paul was added; it stood to the west of Saint-Pierre-le-Majeur. A bit further away, to the southwest of the cathedral, Saint-Gorgon was built in the late eighth century or at the beginning of the next. These constructions clearly demonstrate the links between ecclesiastical power, archi-tecture, and the liturgy. Chrodegang had accompanied Pope Stephen II to the court of Pépin the Short.

A new monastic model emphasizing opulence and prestige appeared in the last twenty years of the eighth century in prominent religious communities such as Centula, or Saint-Riquier, Fulda, Lorsch, and Corvey.

At Saint-Riquier in the Somme, the monastery of Centula was built between 790 and 799 by Angilbert. The abbot of Centula was a member of Charlemagne's court, a poet of renown, and the lover of Charlemagne's daughter Berthe. He summoned the artists and artisans patronised by court dignitaries to build the sumptuous

The development of the westwork
Corvey, near Höxter, Germany, exterior view of the western façade, 873–885. This structure has a true church-porch, with a sanctuary carrying galleries over a porch with vaulted columns. It has lost its central tower, and the wall coping, with the arcades housing the bells, dates from the twelfth century, the spires from the seventeenth. The westwork characterizes Carolingian and Ottonian architecture.

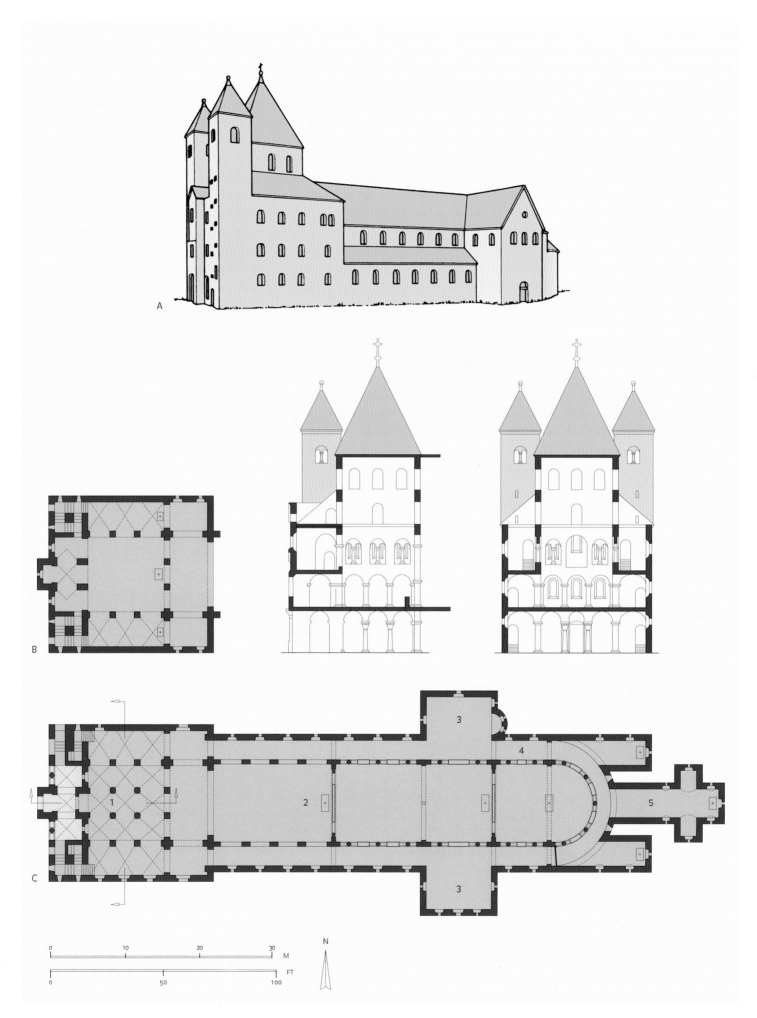

Page 146

The increasing emphasis on height
Corvey, near Höxter, Germany,
873–885.

A Reconstruction of the abbey
 group, without the upper
 gallery or the absidal chapel
 outwork
B Westwork with upper-storey
 plan, longitudinal section, and
 cross section
C Reconstruction of the plan
 1 Ground floor of the
  westwork
 2 Nave with very narrow aisles
 3 Transept
 4 Ambulatory
 5 Cruciform crypt

A gallery of ornamented arcades
Detail of the façade of Corvey,
near Höxter, Germany, 873–885.
Corvey's façade is characterized
by a large, two-storey gallery on
which a protective invocation is
inscribed.

monastic ensemble. The complex is no longer extant and is known to us mainly through the later twelfth-century chronicle of Hariulf. The community of 300 monks moved into a sort of small town, enclosed by fortified walls and towers. The center was a plaza bordered with porticoes (the cloister), which unfolded to the south of the great abbey church consecrated to the Savior and Saint Riquier. The cloister gave onto the church of Saint-Benoît to the east and to that of the Vierge-et-des-Apôtres to the south. The latter is known from excavations, which disclosed a polygonal central plan with ambulatory similar to that of the imperial chapel at Aachen.

The abbey church, consecrated in 799, featured a western choir. Engravings show its exterior appearance and an elevation dominated to the east on both sides of the nave by a transept surmounted by a tower. The entrance led through an *atrium* to a porch in the westwork flanked by two stairway turrets. The ground floor housed relics from the Holy Land, while the altar was placed on a higher level. The fact that the entire community could gather around the altar gives an idea of its ample proportions.

The east tower was dedicated to Saint Riquier, the west to the Savior. These

Classicizing ornament
Detail of capitals from the ground floor of the westwork, Corvey, near Höxter, Germany, 873–885. These capitals are mostly characterized by rough-hewn leaves that display the work of an engraver rather than that of a sculptor. The group nonetheless gives evidence of considerable expertise.

The ground floor of the westwork: a vestibule
Corvey, near Höxter, Germany, interior view of the ground floor of the westwork, 873–885. The central section is covered with groin vaults supported by sturdy columns topped with Corinthian-style capitals. The two aisles, to the north and south, were covered by a simple wooden ceiling.

Page 149
The Carolingian gallery
Corvey, near Höxter, Germany, interior view of the upper church in the westwork, 873–885.
The gallery is surrounded, to the south, west, and north, by aisles surmounted by twin window bays. At the west, the central bay of the gallery includes a kind of balcony, understood as an imperial loge or a platform and intended to hold the altar of the archangel Michael.

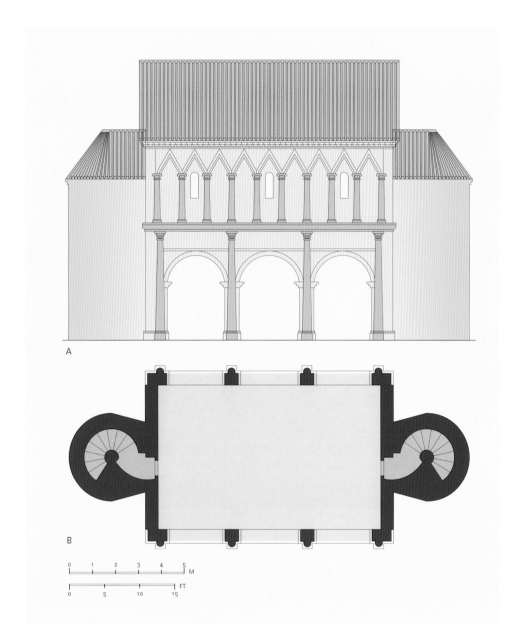

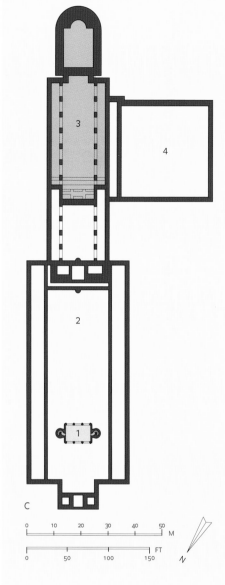

were of the standard Carolingian type, with several compartmented storeys; the altar was on the first floor. In honor of the Trinity, thirty altars (a multiple of three) were distributed throughout the monastery, 300 monks lived there, and the students of the *schola* were divided into three groups of thirty-three each. The significance accorded to the westwork at Saint-Riquier is also found at the monasteries of Lorsch and Minden, the cathedrals of Reims, Hildesheim, and Halberstadt, and, in particular, the monastery of Corvey. This was a distinctive feature of the religious monuments of this period in northern Europe, and remained so until the Romanesque period. The antechurch generally contained a narthex of two or more storeys, a central tower, and two smaller lateral towers; sometimes the beginnings of a nave as well as a counter-choir were included. In addition, certain architectural elements of the Saint-Riquier monastic ensemble recalled Jerusalem's Holy Sepulcher.

The monastery of Corvey, erected between 873 and 885 on the Weser, stood alongside an older basilica. Its plan, with the westwork divided from the nave, flanking aisles and transept, and a large crypt surmounted by an enormous square space, is characteristic; it is also found in the antechurch of the Palatine Chapel in Aachen. The galleries accommodated the singers of the *schola*.

St. Gall, in Switzerland, built at the beginning of the ninth century, illustrates the

Architectural symbol of the Carolingians
Triumphal Gate of Lorsch, Germany, c. 800.
A Elevation of the west façade
B Plan of the Triumphal Gate: two side stairways give access to the rectangular upper room
C Plan of the abbey church of Lorsch with its Triumphal Gate
  1 Triumphal Gate
  2 *Atrium*
  3 Church
  4 Cloister

Commemorated edifice
Triumphal Gate of Lorsch, Germany, view of the west façade, c. 800. The edifice includes an upper-storey room supported on three arches that rest on robust pillars with engaged columns, crowned with composite capitals carrying a sculpted molding. The late Empire triumphal arch commemorates Charlemagne's victory over the Saxons.

Imitation of classical decorative masonry
Detail of the decoration of the upper order ornamenting the Triumphal Gate of Lorsch, Germany. Short, fluted pilasters, topped with Ionic capitals, carry a row of triangular arches. The decorative polychrome blocks of stone begin with square motifs at the ground-floor level and end with an interplay of hexagons: between them runs a row of lozenges.

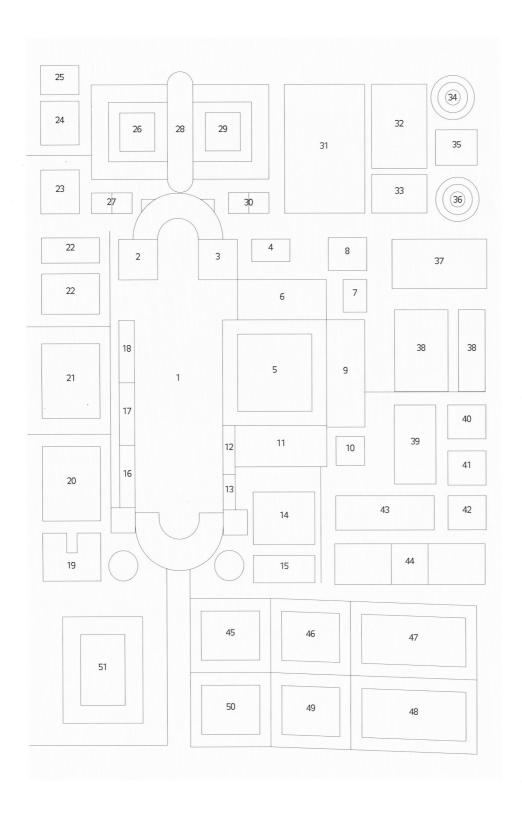

Testimony to Western monastic architecture

The monastic orders became established after the Council of 816–817, meeting at Inden and Aachen. The plan of St. Gall bears witness to this desire for codification and provides an example of the monastic town at the beginning of the ninth century. Reconstructed schematic plan after Werner Vogler.

1 Church, **2** Study room, with library above, **3** Two-storey sacristy, **4** Room where the sacramental elements are prepared, **5** Cloister, **6** Heated day room, with dormitory above, **7** Bath, **8** Latrines, **9** Refectory, with wardrobe above, **10** Kitchen, **11** Cellar below room for storing provisions, **12** Parlor, **13** Space reserved for administrative functions, **14** Residence for pilgrims, **15** Brewery and bakery for pilgrims, **16** Caretaker's lodge, **17** Residence of the abbot, **18** Reception area for visiting monks, **19** Brewery and bakery for the visitors' residence, **20** Visitors' residence, **21** Outer school, **22** Abbey, **23** Leeching, **24** Physician's office, **25** Garden of medicinal plants, **26** Hospital, **27** Kitchen and baths for the hospital and Leeching, **28** Double chapel for the hospital and for novices, **29** Novitiate, **30** Kitchen and bath for the novices, **31** Courtyard for contemplation; orchard, **32** Kitchen garden, **33** Gardener's lodge, **34** Courtyard for geese, **35** Keeper's lodge, **36** Courtyard for chickens, **37** Barn, **38** Workshops, **39** Brewery and bakery for the monks, **40** Mill, **41** Press, **42** Malt kiln, **43** Granary and cooperage, **44** Stalls for bulls and stables, **45** Sheepfold, **46** Goat shed, **47** Stalls for cows, **48** Riding stables, **49** Pigsty, **50** Servants' quarters, **51** Shelter for retinue traveling with nobles

movement toward the codification of monastic architecture (about 820) after the Council of 816–817. A veritable city, this Carolingian monastery is known to us largely through plans and drawings; it was intended to fulfill the spiritual, daily, and material needs of both the community (dormitories, refectories, kitchens, infirmary, cloister, school, and abbot's residence), and of pilgrims and visitors. Symbolically sited at the center of the complex, the church takes up almost half the area of the monastery. The westwork, dedicated to St. Peter, was completed here by a western apse and replaced the more usual western tower. This development of the western section of the church, which is an aspect of *more romano* construction, can be interpreted as a Romanization of the Carolingian liturgy when inspired by Roman models. The crypt discovered under the eastern choir during excavations

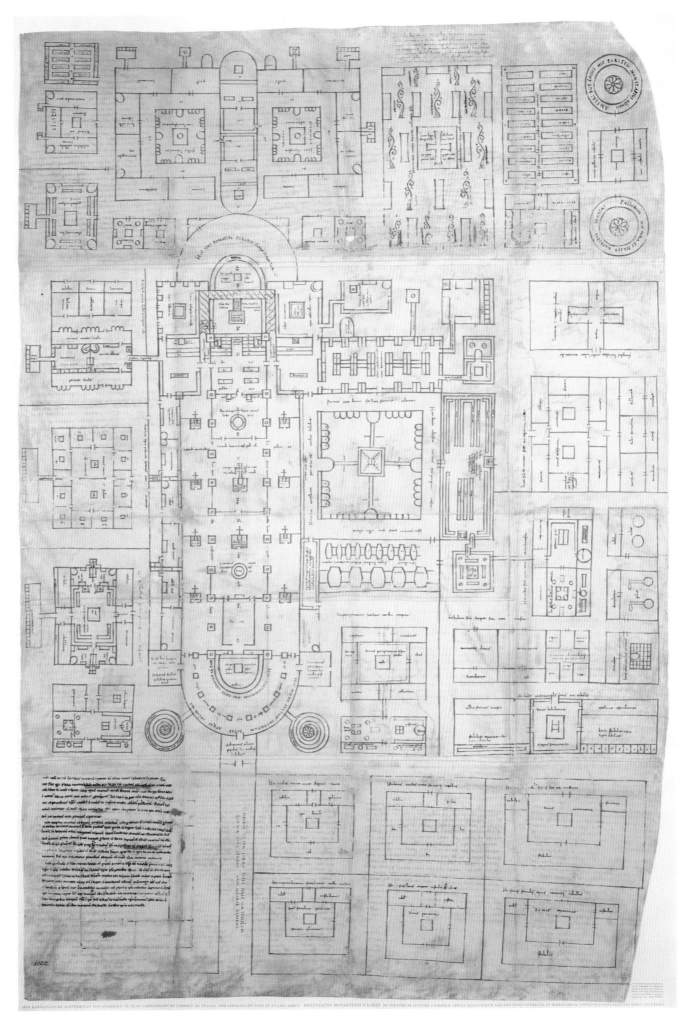

**The key monument of
Ottonian architecture**
Sankt Michael, Hildesheim,
Germany, exterior view of the
western choir, first third of the
eleventh century. There are two
choirs at east and west ends; the
west choir is significantly larger,
resting on a vast apse above a
crypt-hall. It is surrounded by an
ambulatory in which niches
throughout replace the expected
radiating chapels.

Page 153
Project of an ideal plan
St. Gall, Switzerland, plan of the
monastery, beginning of the ninth
century. The plan was drawn with
red ink on a sheet of parchment
containing five pieces sewn
together. Captions written in
brown ink indicate the function of
the different buildings and specify
the furnishings of important
rooms. This precious document
was drawn to a precise scale.
(Library of the abbey, St. Gall,
Cod. Sang. 1092)

confirms the liturgical function served by this section of the abbey church, in contrast with Roman churches, which accorded great importance to western sections.

At Cologne, the cathedral consecrated in 870 was rebuilt by order of the bishop Hiltibald early in the ninth century. Its plan included a western apse doubled by an ambulatory and a monumental western transept of such proportions that it entirely eclipsed the east-end of the church. A similar plan was chosen at Fulda, which drew for its monumental dimensions on the example of old Saint Peter's in Rome.

After the death of Charlemagne, architecture seems to have returned to the more modest dimensions recommended by the Council of Aachen.

Ottonian Architecture

The first ruler of the Holy Roman Empire, Otto I (962–973) turned to Italy in his quest to realize his dream of reconstructing the Carolingian Empire. Historically, Ottonian architecture belongs to the period between the second half of the tenth century and the first quarter of the eleventh, up to the death of Henry II in 1024. However, its influence extended almost to the end of the eleventh century.

The easternmost end of the duchy of Saxony contains the oldest structures, notably, the cathedral of Magdeburg, which probably had two choirs and, as at Fulda, two eastern towers. The church of Sankt Cyriakus of Gernrode (960–965), with a nave flanked by aisles and surmounted by galleries, a transept with two chapels at the east, a westwork that served as the counterapse, as well as the upper part of a crypt at the east, summarizes the characteristics of Ottonian architecture, which also favored alternating supports and wood roofs and ceilings.

Bipolar churches
Sankt Michael, Hildesheim, contains a nave and two aisles, and east and west transepts, each with a central tower and flanked by polygonal stairway turrets. The symmetry of east and west ends makes this one of the most important buildings of the Ottonian period.

Page 157
The rhythms of the nave
Sankt Michael, Hildesheim, Germany, interior view of the nave looking east, first third of the eleventh century. Basilican in type, the rather short nave has a flat ceiling and high windows. Each of its bays is divided by three arcades, with two columns between two pillars. This alternation proved highly popular in Saxony during the Romanesque period.

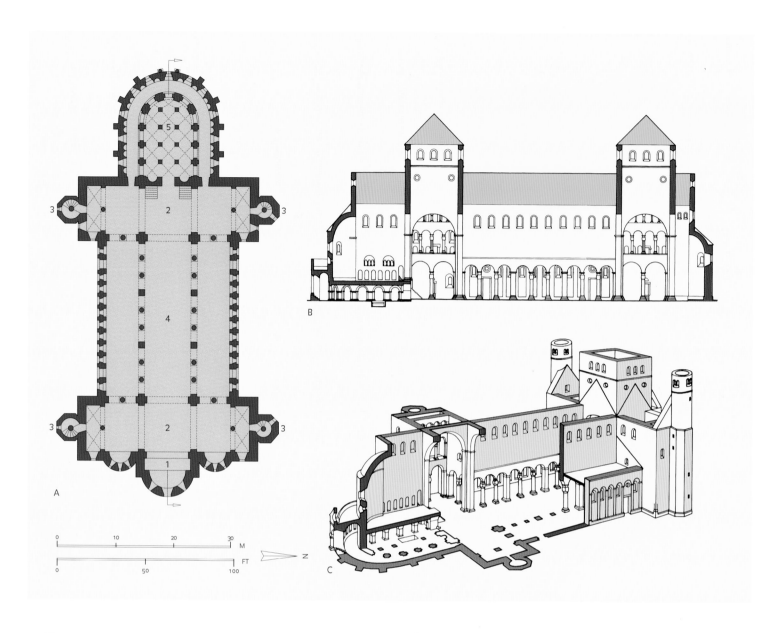

The second quarter of the eleventh century brought a recentering of the basic liturgical ceremonies around the eastern altar. At this time, the internal arrangements of the Carolingian westwork was modified, while its exterior structure remained intact. That of the church of the Trinity at Essen is an imitation of the one in the Palatine Chapel at Aachen, reduced in its dimensions and cut in half in order to assume the appearance of a counterapse opening onto the nave through a large arcade. On the exterior, the formula of an octagonal tower flanked by two lower turrets would be repeated in Lotharingia in the Romanesque period. The westwork of Reims Cathedral likewise displayed a reduction in the internal masses of the Carolingian westwork, as did that of Sankt Pantaleon in Cologne, which nonetheless adopted on the exterior the type featuring a square central tower flanked by appendices incorporated into the arms of the transept, preceded by a deep porch containing two high turrets.

Next came an extension of the choir at the east and a development of the crypts both under the choir and behind the chevet. The eastern apse of the Church of the Trinity at Essen, for example, was extended by an exterior crypt with no fewer than four aisles and a nave. The Carolingian transept took different forms: a continuous transept, with a regular crossing, where the nave and transept intersect at the same height, or a low transept, whose arms virtually serve as lateral chapels. The abbey church of Bad Hersfeld, although in ruins, offers a remarkable illustration of the continuous transept separating the nave and choir.

Similarities between the two ends of the church
Sankt Michael, Hildesheim, Germany, first third of the eleventh century. The east and west ends are similar in both form and volume.
A Plan
    1 East chevet with three apses
    2 Transept topped with a square lantern tower
    3 Polygonal stairway turrets
    4 Nave and aisles
    5 Crypt-hall with ambulatory set with niches throughout
B Longitudinal section
C Axonometric projection

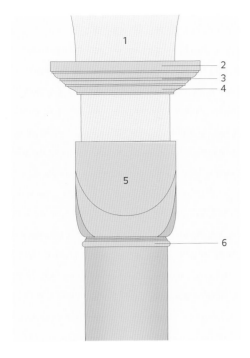

Rough-hewn cube-shaped capital
Detail of the capitals of Sankt
Michael, Hildesheim, Germany,
first third of eleventh century.
These cube-shaped capitals are
crowned by a strongly projecting
abacus. The lower part consists
of a hemisphere from which four
faces are hewn; it is capped with
a cube.
1 Keystone
2 Abacus
3 Molding
4 Bevel
5 Cube-shaped capital
6 Astragal

Among all the surviving structures, the church of Sankt Michael in Hildesheim presents the most thoroughly evolved creation of Ottonian conception in architectural and religious terms. As in the Carolingian abbey church in Centula, the two ends of the nave share equal importance. In a perfect symmetry, each one has a transept topped by a square tower pierced with openings supported by four arcades that come together in the shape of a cross. This solution derived from the Carolingian tradition would find expression in the Romanesque period. The entire edifice pays tribute to the originality of the Ottonian architects, who had fully assimilated the Carolingian heritage, which they joined to traditions of the Italian world. In Rome, the Roman basilical form of the church of San Bartolomeo all Isola, built by Otto II, asserts its continuity with paleo-Christian architecture. On the other hand, the area north of Italy at the very end of the tenth century witnessed the elaboration of the earliest Roman architecture, which in the following century would spread through the south of France and in Catalonia.

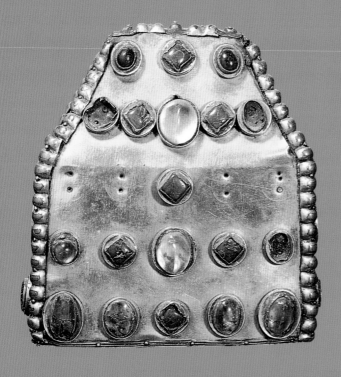

CHARLEMAGNE'S EMPIRE

Tombs and Relics

Page 161

The Merovingian heritage in metalwork
Reliquary of Saints Candida and Eleutherius, ninth century. This reliquary in the form of a purse is decorated with ordinary and semiprecious stones arranged in rows. It offers an excellent example of Carolingian metalwork, which, unlike Carolingian manuscript illumination or ivory carving, remained indebted to Merovingian models. (Trésor de l'Abbaye de Saint-Maurice, Valais)

Anthropomorphic reliquaries
Detail of the head, which dates from the Late Roman Empire, and the back of the throne of the statue-reliquary of Saint Foy, end of the tenth century. This portrait is composed of gold sheet on wood, decorated with precious stones, enamels, and glass beads. A symbolic portrait associated with royal power, it is intended to give an illusion of presence. (Trésor de l'eglise de Sainte-Foy, Conques)

We have noted the importance accorded to tombs and relics in the design and reconstruction of some of the buildings discussed. Reliquaries were the depositories of a cathedral or abbey's spiritual renown; they were also partly responsible for its material well-being as relics attracted pilgrims and offerings.

The relics of martyred saints who had become the object of local or regional cults were highly prized; but the most important of all were those relating to Christ, the Cross, or His tomb, or to the Virgin. The inventory of the relics belonging to the abbey of Saint-Riquier during the Carolingian period has come down to us in Hariulf's *Chronicon Centulense*: "Relics of Our Savior. Wood from the Cross. Of His clothing. Of His sandals. Of His cradle. Of His sponge. Of the water from the Jordan, with which He was baptized. Of the stone where He sat after feeding the five thousand. Of the bread that He distributed to His disciples. Of the temple of the Lord. Of the candle lit at His birth. Of the Mount of Olives. Of His table, where He set at prayer. Of the mountain where He was transfigured. Of the column to which He was tied while He was flogged. Of the rope with which He was tied. Of the stone from which ascended the Cross. Of the nails with which He was crucified. Of earth from Calvary. Of the flask when He was offered gall mingled with vinegar. Of the stone that was pushed away from the entry to His tomb. Of the innocents who, for His sake, suffered martyrdom. Of Mount Horeb. Of wood from the three tabernacles." In addition, He listed the relics of the Virgin ("Of the milk of the Virgin. Of Her hair. Of Her clothing. Of Her cloak"), the apostles, the evangelists, martyrs, confessors, and virgins.

The twenty-five relics of Christ were preserved in the abbey's main reliquary, which became an object of worship. (It was placed in the crypt of the Savior. The crypt was on the ground floor of the westwork, and was built between 790 and 799. Above it, on the first floor, was the altar consecrated to the Savior and the Holy Innocents. This list of relics is eloquent of the rivalry of the most powerful monasteries during the Early Middle Ages. Each attempted to amass the greatest number of relics. It also testifies to the importance of journeys to the Holy Land in search of relics from holy places; there was a thriving trade in relics in the West.

Relics might be acquired at any stage of a monastery's development, but the most important were generally those contributed at the time of the building's consecration; this was especially true of smaller buildings. The relics were placed in shrines or separate reliquaries. Tombs were often placed at the west end of a church. A good example of this disposition is found in the Carolingian cathedral of Reims, begun by Ebbo (817–835) and consecrated by Hincmar in 862; it was modified, and the antechurch crypt reconstructed, by Adalbero.

The "crypt" in such cases was a vaulted ground floor, often surmounted by an oratory with an altar. During the Carolingian period, it was common to place an altar above holy remains at both west and east ends. In that period, one might find, as at Saint-Germain in Auxerre, an altar dedicated to the titular saint that had been placed directly in the lower crypt, but an oratory placed above the tomb was more

The crypt, an essential
element of the Carolingian church
Saint-Victor, Marseilles, Bouches-
du-Rhônes, view of its underground crypt. Its mausoleum, with
groin-vaulted aisles, is preceded
by a portico bordered by a
colonnade on three sides. Of its
decoration, all that remains is a
mosaic with a gold background in
the intrados of an arch, a vine
ornament modeled in the stucco
of the intrados of the arch leading
to the east aisle, and this very
characteristic pillar, crowned with
a sculpted human face.

Above the crypt:
a fortified Romanesque church
The exterior of the basilica of
Saint-Victor, Marseilles, Bouches-
du-Rhônes, presents fortified
substructures dating from the
Romanesque period. Under this
church can be found the crypts of
the High Middle Ages.

Page 165
Tombs of the earliest martyrs
Saint-Victor, Marseilles, Bouches-
du-Rhônes, interior. In the Middle
Ages, a classical building with
nave and two aisles extended to
the south by a square construction
was incorporated into the crypts
of the abbey of Saint-Victor;
seven tombs were housed there,
two of them combined beneath a
single stone framework.

often found. This was true of Saint-Germain and the cathedral of Auxerre, Saint-Médard in Soissons, Saint-Bénigne in Dijon, Flavigny, and elsewhere. At a slightly later period, Helgaud described this custom in relation to Saint-Aignan in Orléans: "Robert [...] undertook to build over his [Aignan's] tomb a house of Our Lord more beautiful than the one already standing there."

Such separate architectural projects were conditional on the presence of a saint who attracted large crowds. The stakes were high, in terms not only of prestige but of income; in certain cases the flood of worshippers was truly considerable. At Saint-Martin in Tours, for example, as early as the Carolingian period, canons were assigned to welcome the pilgrims, whose numbers were so great that some literary texts compared them to the number of pilgrims to Rome. In a diploma of 832, Louis the Pious regulated the distribution of offerings made at the tomb of Saint Martin by the faithful: one-third was to be allocated to the canons, with the exception of precious fabrics, which served to decorate the tomb, and wax and oil, which were used to illuminate the church. Charitable establishments grew up around the basilica to accommodate pilgrims, and the Carolingian monarchs, in memory of their own pilgrimages, donated a lot of money for the reception of pilgrims. The generous donor might hope to be interred near the holy remains, as indicated by an epitaph of 851: "Here lies Bodolaïcus of virtuous reputation, whose soul, we believe, is in repose due to the pious treasure of his alms and his love for Saint Martin. He

The tomb – place of pilgrimage
Crypt of Saint-Germain, Auxerre, mid-ninth century. The tomb occupies the centre of early medieval crypts; around them extends the complex of corridors through which pilgrims circulated.

died in peace the eighth day of the calends of September, in the twelfth year of King Charles."

Relics were sometimes divided up so that the number of sanctuaries within the building could be multiplied, creating a *martyrium*. We have already mentioned, in this context, the phenomenon of lower and upper crypts, but, more generally, the evolution of the worship of relics beginning with the Carolingian period tended toward their distribution in different sanctuaries within the same church.

In 852 in Reims, the archbishop Hincmar withdrew the remains of Saint Rémi from their stone sarcophagus and placed them in a silver *loculus,* housed in the *crypta* that had just been built. He carefully set aside the shroud, depositing it in an ivory reliquary in order to create a second relic. With less solicitude, the abbot Étienne of Tournus in 969 divided the bones of Saint Valerian, which had just been discovered in the sarcophagus; the head, enclosed in an *imago,* was placed in the sanc-

In the crypt of Saint-Germain
Detail of the masonry of the wall
and a frieze in the crypt of Saint-
Germain, Auxerre, mid-ninth
century.

tuary of the main church, while a *scrinium* (reliquary) containing the rest of the bones was deposited in the crypt *(inferius oratorium)*. This was an old practice, attested in 845 at Saint-Riquier, when the head of the saint was separated from the body and deposited in a wooden reliquary, replaced in 864 by a silver reliquary enriched with gold and precious stones. Under Charles the Bald, the relics of Sainte Foy of Conques had been divided between a *capsa* and an *imago*. This apportionment of relics between the lower crypts and the main church exercised considerable influence over the development of religious architecture and led to an increase in the production of reliquaries made out of precious metals.

It led first and foremost to the proliferation of crypts, especially in collegiate and abbey churches. There were three basic types: subterranean, half underground, or outside the east-end. Crypts were reached via stairs and corridors leading from paired doors in the aisles or the arms of the transept. They were generally

Page 168
The Carolingian crypt redisigned for the cult of relics
Saint-Germain, Auxerre, perspective view of the reliquary shrine, mid-ninth century. The central space of the crypt is connected to corridors that run around it in order to facilitate the circulation of pilgrims. Pictured here is a corridor joining the axial chapel and the chevet. It is covered with groined vaults resting on massive pillars.

positioned directly under the upper sanctuary and its altar, to which they gave structural support. Housing the relic, these *martyrium* crypts had the symbolic function of a monumental reliquary that protected the tomb (or its representative: the worked gold reliquary). The two doors facilitated circulation; the pilgrims entered on one side and exited on the other having touched the tomb or reliquary and been sprinkled with holy water. The latter point is confirmed by both contemporary accounts and archaeological research, which has uncovered wells in many crypts.

As this sanctuary for the worship of the dead was often half-underground, the level of the choir could be raised and openings be pierced in its floor to give a view of the tomb or reliquary in the crypt. The multiplication of relics and the need for easy circulation explain the need for an ambulatory as a corridor surrounding the central shrine. The ambulatory opened out onto chapels marking the successive stages of the pilgrim's visit. Here again, the formula dates from the Carolingian period and reached its culminating point around the year 1000 in Auxerre, Flavigny, Clermond-Ferrand, and Tours. A special branch of architecture developed, whose function it was to enlarge the sanctuary and multiply the number of altars; this was by building crypts beyond the east-end. Such crypts surrounded the east-end entirely and allowed the pilgrims to circulate past a center of devotional intensity situated underground and to the east of the choir. This architectural solution was adopted in the crypts of Saint-Germain of Auxerre and Saint-Pierre of Flavigny, and later, about 1000, in those of Saint-Bénigne de Dijon.

The search for the best way to protect treasures and precious objects led to new and specific architectural genres. According to the *Testament de Charlemagne,* the sovereign's precious objects were divided between three different places: the imperial fortune in precious metals, and perhaps also the ornaments of the *vestiarium,* were kept in the *camera;* precious books in the *bibliotheca;* and objects, books, and *ornamenta* of liturgical kind in the *capella.* In the plan for an ideal monastery at St. Gall, special upper-storey spaces were provided for this purpose and occupying adjoining buildings. Surviving examples of this genre are the *Cámera santa* in

Richly paved floors
Detail of the floor paving of Saint-Germain, Auxerre, mid-ninth century. It shows a fine example of the *opus sectile* used in religious edifices in the Carolingian period.

The Carolingian artistic renaissance in wall painting
Saint-Germain, Auxerre, interior, mid-ninth century. The edifice is decorated with paintings employing the classical *trompe-l'œil* technique and using only earth tones. Those of the walls of the chapel of Saint Stephen depict the protomartyr in front of the Sanhedrin, his arrest and Lapidation. Saints are also pictured on the outside walls of the *confessio*.

Oviedo, which was constructed by the Asturian king, Alfonso II and which dates from the beginning of the ninth century, and the much renovated *Sancta sanctorum* chapel of the Lateran in Rome. Others are known to us only from contemporary sources.

There are many instances of Carolingian constructions or renovations designed to accommodate tombs. In France, Saint-Denis, Saint-Laurent in Grenoble, and Saint-Philibert in Grandlieu suggest the variety of solutions adopted. The dates of the still extant buildings at Saint-Philibert are much discussed. Under Louis the Pious, a new abbey was built about 818 in Déas, not far from Nantes. It was of cruciform plan; the side-aisles it once possessed have since been destroyed. The partly preserved transept separated the nave from a large apse flanked by two absidioles. In 836, the abbot Hibold transferred the tomb of Saint Philibert from the choir to the crypt, which he rebuilt. The extended apse was independent of the two equally deep absidioles. Below the upper choir, the *confessio* comprised access corridors and a series of rooms, probably to the same level as the nave. This arrangement was, however, modified during the Romanesque period.

At Saint-Laurent in Grenoble, a small mausoleum built outside the walls of the

Iconographic program
The wall decoration of Saint-Germain, Auxerre, exhibits geometric patterns and the juxtaposition of plan color. Dark tones, especially ochers, predominate. The surviving ornamentation suggests a decor combining wall painting and stuccos to represent as iconographic program of houses, churches, and funerary structures.

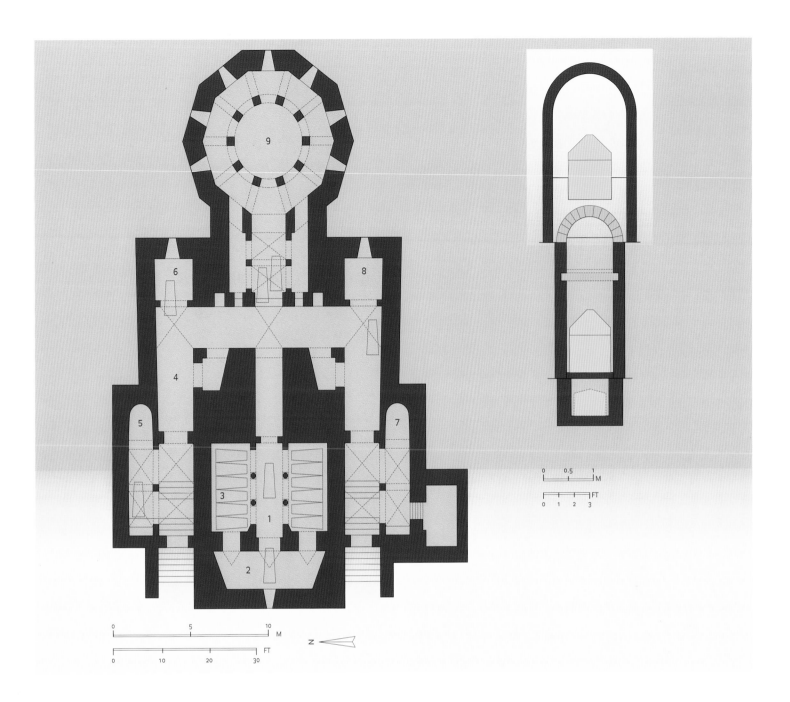

A circular-plan oratory
Crypt, Saint-Germain, Auxerre, like a small basilica with nave and two aisles. At the east is a polygonal rotunda containing a staircase to a lower chapel with three combined sanctuaries.
Left: Early plan of the crypt
1 *Confessio,* 2 Counterapse originally housing the body of Saint Germanus, 3 Sarcophagi with the relics of Saint Germanus and the holy bishops of Auxerre, 4 Ambulatory, 5 Chapel dedicated to Saint Stephen, 6 Chapel of Saint Benedict, 7 Chapel of Saint Lawrence, 8 Chapel of Saint Martin, 9 Rotunda
Right: Cross section

ancient city was rebuilt with a funerary chamber during the Carolingian period. It offers a fine example of a kind of small-scale edifice found throughout the empire. A rectangular nave, covered with a barrel vault, opens to west and east on low apses, flanked on the eastern end by two lateral apses in a trilobed plan. Large arcades enliven the side walls of the nave, carried by three columns crowned by re-used Corinthian capitals. The apse has stucco decoration, a feature we have already noted at Germigny-des-Prés.

One of the principal Carolingian monuments of northern France was the basilica of Saint-Denis. Recent excavations have substantially improved our knowledge of the building. It was a funerary basilica, built during the fifth century in an existing necropolis. During the Merovingian period, it accommodated the princely tombs of Dagobert and his queen Mathilde, Clovis II, and Arnégonde, the wife of Clovis I (she died between 565 and 570). Having been enlarged by Dagobert, the abbey of Saint-Denis was then reconstructed by the abbot Fulrad and solemnly consecrated in 775. It had a basilical plan with the nave divided into nine bays carried on columns. A projecting transept preceded the semicircular apse of the east end; below, a crypt with ambulatory housed the tomb of Saint Denis.

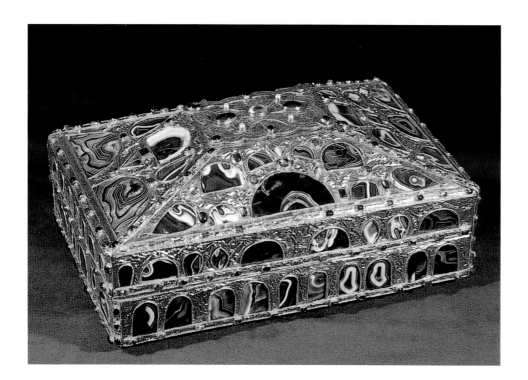

Asturian goldsmiths work: a courtly art
Agate casket, tenth century. The lid of this reliquary is in the shape of a truncated pyramid. It is decorated with re-used enamels and displays areas of exposed agate alongside an overlay of repoussé gold leaf forming "arcades". (Tesoro de la Cámara Santa, Oviedo)

**The appearance of
the statue-reliquary**
Statue-reliquary of Sainte-Foy,
last quarter of the tenth century.
Height: 85 cm; width: 36 cm;
height of throne: 60 cm. Much
gold was added in the late tenth
century. The crystal spheres of
the chair posts date from the
fourteenth century. The glitter of
this anthropomorphic reliquary
made a strong impression on the
crowds who saw the image of the
venerated saint at the east end of
the basilica of Conques. (Trésor de
l'église de Sainte-Foy, Conques)

Page 172 below left
**A marvelous artefact
from a distant age**
"Saint Martin's Vase", c. seventh–
eighth century. Made of sardonyx
that dates from the age of the
Ptolemies, it is set in a gold-work
reliquary decorated with filgree
and cabochons. (Trésor de
l'Abbaye de Saint-Maurice
d'Agaune, Valais)

Page 172 below right
**Offerings of gold
to the Church in Asturias**
The base of the agate casket
carries the following inscription:
"Offered in 910 by Froila and
Nunilo to the church of San
Salvador in Oviedo". Around a
central cross pattée, the ox, the
eagle, the lion, and the figure of a
man (the symbols of the Evangelists), are depicted above the
wheels described in the first
chapter of Ezekiel, explaining
their celestial mobility. (Tesoro
de la Cámara Santa, Oviedo)

Under the abbot Hilduin (814–841), the crypt was extended to create a three-
nave chapel which was consecrated to the Virgin in 832. The reconstruction of such
a large crypt was typical of the Carolingian period. At the west end there was a
counter-choir with polygonal apse that may have contained the tomb of Pépin. The
elevation of the main façade is not known. Excavations have uncovered column-
bases sculpted with foliage motifs, which suggest that the royal abbey was richly
decorated. Saint-Denis was the scene of some of the key moments of the Merovingian dynasty: the burial of Charles Martel, the crowning of Pépin by Pope Stephen
II in 754, the papal benediction of Charlemagne and his brother Carloman, and the
burial of Pépin.

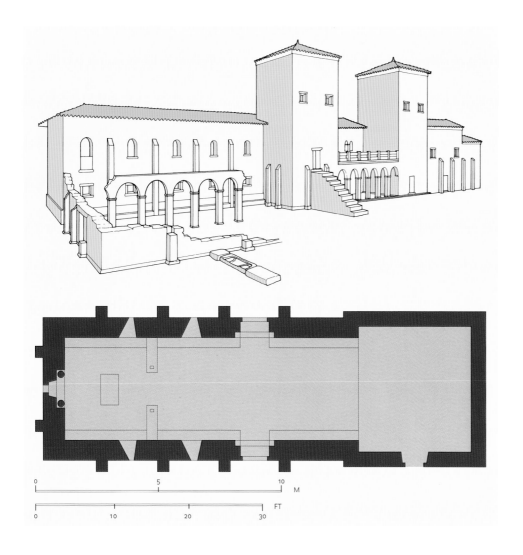

Burgundian Experiments

The Burgundian basilicas of Saint-Germain at Auxerre, Saint-Pierre at Flavigny, and
Saint-Bénigne at Dijon – the last of these dates from the early Romanesque period
– perfectly illustrate the evolution of Carolingian architecture. These buildings
testify to the progressive enlargement of the chevet. The architecture of the east
end grew increasingly complex as two superposed crypts were added, each of them
with lateral corridors.

From the fifth century, the city of Auxerre, defended by walls built in the previ-
ous century, possessed numerous sanctuaries; the most important was the basilica
of the Abbaye Saint-Germain, named after the bishop who administered the diocese from 418 to 448. Between 840 and 860, the comte d'Argovie, Charles the Bald's
uncle, endowed the embellishment and enlargement of the monastery of Saint-
Germain. He made it the center of an influential school that was placed under the
direction of, first Haymon, then Héric († about 880). It was a center of intense intellectual activity whose influence reached as far as Laon, Reims, and Paris in the tenth
century, through the work Héric's, Rémi of Auxerre († 908).

Not far from the prestigious Merovingian basilica in which Saint Germain
reposed, queen Clotilde had founded a monastery. This was rebuilt between 841
and 859, at the instigation of the miraculously cured abbot Conrad. It was consecrated on Epiphany of 859; the service was attended by Charles the Bald. Héric's
book, the *Miracles de Saint Germain,* written at some date prior to 876, records the
construction process. Of this sumptuous Carolingian abbey church, nothing remains
but the very spacious and complex crypt. The central part is like a a subterranean
basilica, with short, barrel-vaulted nave and aisles, separated by columns sur-

mounted by wooden architraves which rest on the capitals. Various sarcophagi were housed here, while the remains of Saint Germain were kept in a western apse.

In 887, new access corridors were built and the tomb of Saint Germain moved to the crypt complex. The angled corridors of the ambulatory were symmetrically arranged around the axis of the abbey, opening on two chapels, the north chapel consecrated to the Saints Étienne and Benoît and the south to Saints Laurent and Martin. In the chapel of Saint-Étienne, wall paintings retrace scenes from the life of the saint.

Further east, following the axes of the abbey, a rectangular passage divided into nave and aisles leads to a central-plan chapel with an annular ambulatory. Its date remains controversial. Several stairways giving access to the upper choir complete the complex. At crypt level, in the eastern rotunda, a stairway led down to a lower crypt consecrated to Pope Clement, saint and martyr. The three floors of the choir in the easternmost section, the chapels set along the processional palt (the technical term is *apse échelon*), and the scale of the crypt chamber, all typical features of the new Carolingian model, give us an idea of the imposing appearance once

Monuments for holy bodies
Saint-Laurent, Grenoble, view of the excavations, second half of the fifth–seventh century. Around a central room of square plan are set four trilobed annexes each comprising three unconnected apses of similar dimensions (the west branch has only two). The discovery of trapezoidal sarcophagi attests the funerary function of this building, one of the more important medieval religious sites.

Decorated walls frame the volumes
Saint-Laurent, Grenoble, view of the crypt, second half of the fifth–seventh century. The crypt of Saint Oyend features a decoration of stone and brick, and, surrounding the nave, a colonnade; this carries the lintels from which rise the barrel vault and the arches that frame the axial apses. The liturgical function of this edifice is shown by the fine decoration and the two access stairways to promote the circulation of pilgrims.

assumed by this Burgundian basilica, whose influence can be traced in the architecture of Flavigny.

Attracted by the abbey's prosperity during the ninth century, the city expanded to the north, and houses surrounded the monastery. A Viking siege at the end of the ninth century, in 887, and another in 910 curbed this growth – the suburban sanctuaries were set on fire and destroyed. Deeply shaken, the city of Auxerre reorganized its defenses. Saint-Germain was fortified in the early tenth century, while other buildings, such as the abbey of Sainte-Marie, on the far bank of the River Yonne, were restored only much later (in the case of Sainte-Marie, in the twelfth century).

Carolingian architecture in Burgundy is known essentially through the crypts of Saint-Germain of Auxerre and the abbey of Saint-Pierre in Flavigny. In the eighth century, Flavigny housed the relics of Saint Prix, the bishop of Clermont, and Saint Amarin; then, in the ninth century the body of Reine, virgin, and martyr, was added. The old abbey of Saint-Pierre was rebuilt by Abbot Egil to accomodate these remains, and the new abbey consecrated by Pope John VIII in 878. The presence of seven altars at the east end gives an indication of the scale of the structure, which was altered in the Romanesque period.

Its plan came to light thanks to excavations, which revealed a crypt complex similar to that of Saint-Germain. A central-plan chapel, in the axis but behind the chevet, was connected to the apse-*martyria* by three short hallways, separated by arcades resting on pillars. The apse was semicircular on the interior and polygonal on the exterior. Around this an ambulatory was built slightly later (878). Beyond the ambulatory were two lateral absidioles. Of the architectural decor of the crypt, five pillars survive, one of them in the southern corridor; their interlace pattern and floral ornamentation relate them to contemporary Italian sculpture.

At Saint-Pierre in Flavigny, an early version of the eastern apse was similar in principle and appearance to a rotunda set in the axis; during the Romanesque period, it became hexagonal. This architectural development culminated in Saint-Bénigne at Dijon. Its rotunda, erected by Abbot William of Volpiano between 1001 and 1017, was placed in the easternmost section of the basilica. The Sainte-Marie rotunda rose three storeys high behind the chevet of the abbey church. The lower floor communicated directly with the underground crypt and the middle floor with the ground floor of the church. Two round towers, north and south, provided access between levels. The the two lower storeys had concentric colonnades; the third storey was crowned by a bombé dome.

Saint-Germain in Auxerre and Saint-Pierre in Flavigny illustrate early stages of a development whose culmination is the Sainte-Marie rotunda in Dijon. The last-named undoubtedly set the stage for the ambulatory choirs that became widespread in France from the second quarter of the ninth century.

The architectural formulae created by the builders of the Carolingian Empire can thus be seen as decisive in the passage of the art of the Early Middle Ages to Romanesque. The abbey church of Cluny II, for example, adopted the St. Gall plan as late as 1045. St. Gall may even have influenced the architects of Fontenay in the twelfth century. The influence of Carolingian architecture also made itself felt in the churches of Reichenau, in, for example, Sankt Georg at Oberzell (late ninth or early tenth century). In Germany, the Carolingian style gave way to Ottonian architecture under the new dynasty of Otto I. In other regions, a logical and continuous progression between pre-ninth-century buildings and those of the tenth and eleventh centuries is less discernible.

An Italian connection in the sculpted decoration

Detail of a capital from the crypt of Saint-Oyend, Saint-Laurent, Grenoble, second half of the fifth–seventh century. The capitals of limestone or re-used marble are topped with thick abaci ornamented with foliage. This decoration owes nothing to either the classical period or to the Late Roman Empire; instead, it is related to chancels of eighth-century northern Italy.

Partial reconstruction of the fifth–seventh century church

This plan of the crypt of Saint-Laurent, Grenoble, includes the east and west arms of the Merovingian church.

1 North apse of the crypt
2 East apse of the crypt
3 South apse of the crypt
4 West apse of the chapel
5 Symmetrical corridors permitting access to the crypt
6 Side apses of the west arm of the Merovingian cruciform-plan church

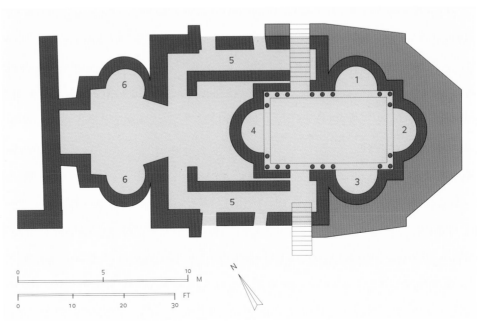

Dark but highly ornamented crypts
Saint-Bénigne, Dijon, Burgundy, interior view of the crypt, beginning of the eleventh century. The very large crypt is circular in plan, corresponding to the rotunda that formerly stood over it. Its capitals offer a form of rough-hewn Corinthian-style decoration obtained by a simply cutting away the corners, but it also has capitals with carved foliage into which other motifs, such as the figure of man shown here, are incorporated.

Liturgy and Architecture in the Carolingian Period

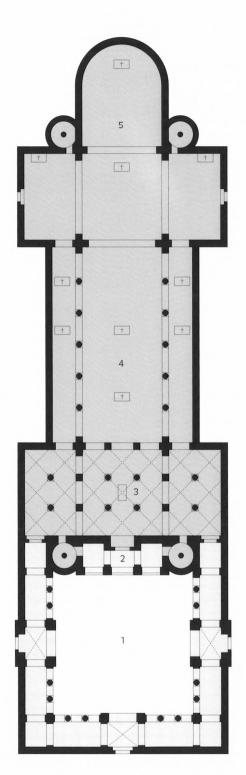

The liturgy comprises a certain number of ceremonies and prayers, whose order differs in the different churches. During the Carolingian period, the stational liturgy served partly itinerant ceremonies; on certain days, the "station" days, bishops and clergy processed from one church to another to the "station" church where the service was held.

The monastery of Centula or Saint-Riquier hosted numerous processions, some daily and some exceptional, which circulated between the two poles of the abbey complex, Saint-Riquier to the east and Saint-Sauveur to the west. On the way, the procession stopped many times at altars where readings were given or prayers were offered. This peripatetic liturgy filled the churches twice a day, for matins and vespers. This was typical of the Carolingian liturgy, whose origins in the Gallican tradition resulted in a liturgy rich in processions. It was also marked by certain Roman arrangements introduced in the late eighth and early ninth century by Alcuin. The Carolingian liturgy was in use over a fixed period of history and within a limited geographical area. Recent excavations have confirmed the bipolarity of the abbey church. The tower of the Savior at Saint-Riquier was an octagonal ground floor with a raised fondation, identical to the Palatine Chapel in Aachen. In this context, the nave was first and foremost an area in which the various processions required by the liturgy found their place.

This bipolarity can also be seen in Fulda. The abbey church was built there in the early ninth century in imitation of Saint Peter's in Rome; its architectural and liturgical focus is its west end, whose *more romano* chevet was placed under the protection of Saint Peter; it faced the choir dedicated to the Savior. The liturgical function of the counter-apse imports a liturgical and monumental symmetry similar to that of Saint-Riquier.

In Auxerre, architecture, liturgy, and culture converged in the Carolingian period. The masters of Auxerre actively participated in the major currents of thought in the second half of the ninth century. Like all the intellectuals of the period, they were interested in Neoplatonism and fascinated by Antiquity. In the framework of the Carolingian imperial renaissance, the artistic centers of Auxerre sought useful examples and materials they could update and restore to use.

The crypts of Saint-Germain in Auxerre illustrate these intellectual currents; the capitals, for example, were imitations of classical capitals. The *scriptorium* (a room set apart for writing or copying manuscripts) and the study of classical texts inspired a choice of decor copied from profane works and evocative of Imperial Rome. But the masters of Auxerre were very much of their own time too. The crypts, designed in or around 840, show an in-depth knowledge of most of the major architectural innovations of the preceding two decades. Thus, the crypts moved from simple annular design to a much more intricate use of space, with an entire complex developing around the small, central room reserved for the holy relics. Access to the relics in the crypts was originally through narrow corridors which were unsuitable for processions by large numbers. Probably under the influence of the processional liturgy, the corridors were replaced by a series of altars, each with their own place in the rite and their own independent oratory; the crypt complexes expanded to accomodate this arrangement.

Strict rules
Plan of the church of Centula, 790–799. From the beginning of the Carolingian period, the transformation of the liturgical rules led to a modification of the very structure of monastic churches. The church of Centula reflected these changes perfectly.

1 Courtyard surrounded by porticoes
2 The west *turris* framed by the stairway turrets
3 Lateral resembling the arms of transepts
4 Nave and aisles with numerous altars
5 Apse

THE APPROACHING MILLENIUM

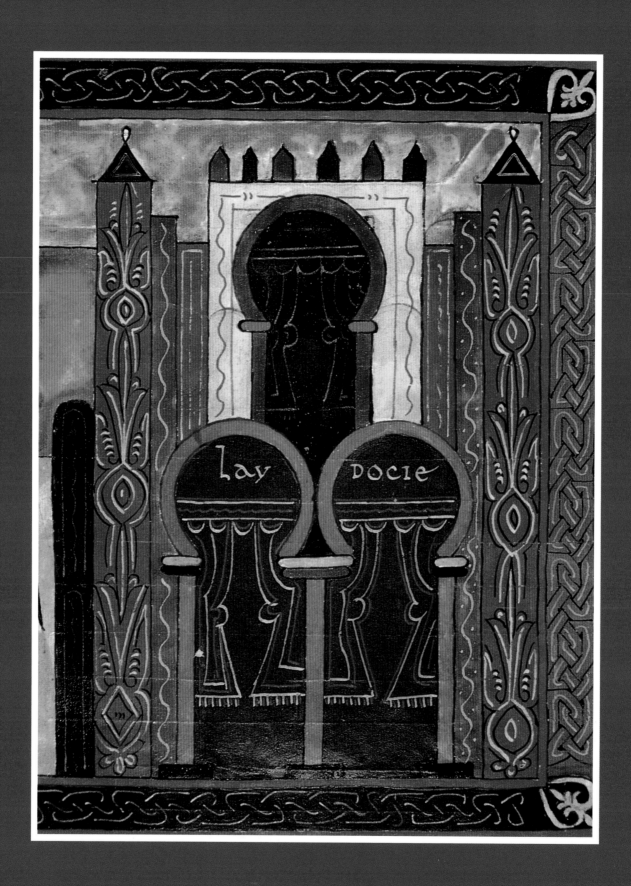

From the North to the Mediterranean

The Peripheral Regions of the North and West

Throughout the eighth and ninth centuries, the Empire experienced turmoil in its outermost territories. These can be divided into three areas: the first of Mediterranean influence, the second defined by the basin of the Rhine, the Danube, and a section of Gaul, and the last including the Scandinavians, the eastern and western Slavs, and the Baltic and Finnish peoples. Beyond these areas lay the Bulgarian Empire, the heptarchy (the seven kingdoms of Anglo-Saxon England), Viking Scandinavia, and the regions of eastern Europe, including Grand Moravia and Kiev. Among the major currents of the period, the struggle of the Danes against the Frankish empire and that of the western Slavs should not be omitted. The various records and accounts of the period always focus on the dependent relationship of these different regions with the Carolingian empire, neglecting their autonomy from a historic as well as cultural point of view. In reality, the organization of the peripheral states of the Frankish kingdom, like that of Anglo-Saxon England or the Asturian kingdom, was based on self-defense with the goal of preserving their independence.

The Anglo-Saxon world in the British Isles maintained a solid and profitable relationship, on an intellectual and political level, with the Frankish kingdom, while retaining authority over its own territory. Within this world, however, kingdoms fought one another in a perpetual struggle for power. In 757 the king of Mercia, Offa, succeeded in establishing a political hegemony that lasted until 796. It remained unequaled until the reign of Alfred the Great, king of Wessex (871–899), who in 871 drove out the Scandinavians who had been living in Wessex since 865.

The cultural and political influence of the Carolingian court was widely felt in the Anglo-Saxon kingdoms. Moreover, Aethelwulf reinforced relations with the continent by marrying the daughter of Charles the Bald, Judith. During the reign of his son, Alfred the Great (whose story is well known thanks to his biographer, Bishop Asser) these ties grew stronger; evidence for this is provided by illuminated manuscripts such as the Chester-le-Street Evangelistary, written in Carolingian miniscule about 900, and by religious art in general.

Very few traces remain of the architecture that predates the Norman period, in which new monuments were built and old ones demolished. Some churches were made of wood, like that of Greenstead in Essex, following the Nordic tradition. A more representative example of the Anglo-Saxon heritage is found at Bradford-on-Avon. It features irregularly shaped blocks of cut stone, solid cornerstones, and has a porch in the façade. The arches at Bradford-on-Avon continue slightly beyond the semi-circular without becoming full horseshoe arches.

However, Anglo-Saxon religious architecture also made use of perfectly regular stonework. The most commonly adopted plan was a nave without aisles extended by a rectangular east end, lower and narrower than the nave, and, flanked by two small rooms. This plan seemes already to have been in use by the seventh century in England, as attested by the excavations at Saint Oswald's Minster in Gloucester.

Prefiguration of the sculpted art of the medieval West
The Cross of the Scriptures of Clonmacnois, County Offaly, Ireland, first half of the tenth century. This stone cross displays interlace and scroll motifs interspersed with scenes from the life of Christ. The tradition of sculpting figures in the British Isles is amply demonstrated in its broad iconographic program, and foreshadow the monumental sculpture of the Middle Ages.

Another characteristic of British architecture of the ninth century is the frequent placement of an apse on the western side of the edifice, as in continental Carolingian architecture. Thus, the plan of Canterbury, which probably had two apses, may well have been influenced by the Germanic world. This plan was also used for Saint Oswald's Minster, whose western section, dating from the Early Middle Ages, is akin to the Carolingian model. A ninth-century second apse is also found in Saint Mary's in Castro, at Dover.

From Late Antiquity on, sustained contacts between England and Ireland ensured that the influence of Irish civilization was strongly felt. These contacts reached their height in the sixth and seventh centuries. During the seventh and eighth centuries, Irish religious architecture underwent an evolution that benefited from the great Irish monastic expansion in the direction of not only England but the continent. The island itself experienced a notable growth of monasticism, in which veritable monastic cities replaced the original hermitages. So large were these settlements that a core of population gathered around the tiny original foundations, themselves giving rise to towns capable of carrying on trade with England and the continent.

Toward the end of the eighth century, Ireland also evolved an architecture using wood, represented, for example, by the church of Saint Brigid in Kildare, constructed in 868 by order of Queen Flanna. According to original sources, a large proportion of the workers assigned to the construction had as their exclusive task the cutting of trees and preparation of wood. Nonetheless, the use of stone did not

Faith through asceticism
Saint Kevin's Church,
Glendalough, County Wicklow,
Ireland, exterior, end of the
thirteenth century. Ireland's stone
constructions are rectangular
with two *antae* at the ends, a door
set high, and one or more round
towers. The isolated location of
this church is powerfully evocative
of the eremitic and monastic life
of Irish monks.

disappear, as seen in the cathedral of Glendalough at the end of the eighth century. The most popular plan was a simple rectangle with rooms at the ends, one or more round towers, and a door above floor-height.

In the northern part of the continent, far from the seat of Carolingian power, the Christian states of the Scandinavian world – Sweden, Denmark, Norway – did not attain stability until the end of the tenth century. Their culture is known to us primarily through tombs, like that of Oseberg in Norway, which enclosed a boat about 22 m long, and of Jellinge in Denmark, which contained jewels and fibulae. Both of these funerary monuments were marked with a stone carved with resolutely Christian iconography.

Although it goes slightly beyond the period dealt with in this book, it is worth mentioning that the Viking civilization left its mark in fortified monuments in south Denmark, on the very edges of the European continent. Of the most important of these fortresses – Trelleborg, Aggersborg, Fyrkat, and Nonnebakken – some were made of stone but most of wood and earth. The fortress of Trelleborg in Sweden, on the Baltic coast, comprised an inner encampment protected by a circular wall and a moat and an outer encampment of wood and earth, surrounded by a second moat. Grid-pattern streets crossing at right angles are lined with houses in groups of four. Archaeological excavations have made possible the identification of a style of domestic architecture belonging to the ninth and tenth centuries, consisting of residences of elongated plan which present a kind of synthesis of styles of Viking civil architecture.

Southern Traditions

The architectural models originated in Italy during Late Antiquity exerted great influence over the Carolingian Early Middle Ages, and sovereigns sought to reestablish an imperial status. The crucial role played by the church of San Vitale in Ravenna in the development of the Carolingian Palatine Chapel of Aachen illustrates these influences perfectly.

The substantial trade between Gaul and northern Italy and the establishment of Frankish monasteries in northern Italy promoted artistic interchange. Thus, superposed orders of columns and colonettes, like those of Saint-Laurent in Grenoble or Germigny-des-Prés, undoubtedly had their origins in Lombardy. Another example of interpenetration is the formula of the trilobed east end, wed in the crypt of the monastery of San Salvatore in Brescia, which was founded in 753; this subsequently became widespread in the westernmost areas of Europe.

At Cividale, a major Lombard center, the oratory of Santa Maria in Valle, a small construction with a rectangular plan dating from the end of the eighth century, possesses an important monumental decoration of polychrome stucco that depicts figures in high relief as well as geometric and plant motifs. The style of the reliefs – variously dated from the end of the eighth century to the beginning of the tenth – suggests a Byzantine influence in Lombardy.

The Carolingian period proved particularly brilliant in Rome due to the symbiosis between the strong paleo-Christian traditions and the many restorations and architectural innovations. A great deal of rebuilding was required by the transfer of holy relics from suburban edifices to older monuments inside the city walls.

A vanished material: stucco
San Salvatore, Brescia, Italy, interior, eighth century. The nave of the church is roofed in timber, and separated from the aisles by large barrel-vaulted arcades resting on fluted columns crowned with mostly re-used capitals. Its most distinctive feature is its decoration, which combines very varied motifs modeled in stucco with wall paintings in bright colors.

An interior reflecting Byzantine tradition

Santa Maria in Valle, Cividale, Italy, interior view from the choir toward the back of the façade, c. 780. The rich decoration of the chapel is composed of marble plaques at the lower level and stucco reliefs and frescoes in the upper part.

Lombard architecture in northern Italy

Santa Maria in Valle, Cividale, Italy, plan and cross section, c. 780. The structure comprises a high central mass, square in shape and covered with Roman-style groin vaulting, which adjoins a rectangular choir.

1 Groin-vaulted central room
2 Rectangular choir divided by columns into three chapels

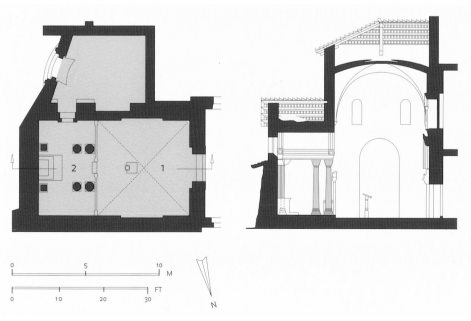

At the beginning of the ninth century, Pope Paschal I (817–824) showed himself a remarkable builder: he seems to have been the initiator of numerous restorations, in particular, in the highly venerated basilicas of Santa Prassede, Santa Cecilia in Trastevere, and Santa Maria in Domnica. Churches with basilical plan (with nave and flanking aisles) remained the model of choice for patrons as is shown by the basilicas of San Giovanni a Porta Latina or Santa Maria in Cosmedin. A strong tendency towards long naves is evident. The *triclinium* of the Lateran Palace is attributed to the pontificate of Leo III (795–816), and the reconstruction of San Marco to Pope Gregory IV (827–844).

The sanctuary of Saint Peter's in Rome made it the most imitated model in the West. In Rome, its plan and elevation were repeated at Santa Prassede, which features an elevation with columns and architraves, a barely projecting transept cross-

A return to partitioned space
Santa Maria in Valle, Cividale, Italy, interior view of the choir, c. 780. Rectangular in plan, the choir is divided into three chapels by means of columns that support architraves on which rest three small barrel vaults. The capitals, derived from the Corinthian order, are similar to those of the *ciborium* in the baptistery of Calixtus (mid-eighth century).

The sculptural treatment of figures in high relief
Detail of the stuccos on the rear of the façade of Santa Maria in Valle, Cividale, Italy, c. 780. The archivolts are ornamented with vines, interlace patterns, and arabesques. Above a painted frieze can be seen the notably elongated bodies of stucco figures similar to those of martyrs having received their crowns of victory, glory, and chastity from Christ.

ing, and a semicircular crypt. There is a nave with side-aisles. The influence of the plan of Saint Peter's continued throughout the Carolingian period thanks to its exceptionally high symbolic status; early in the Romanesque period, the large monastery of Santa María de Ripoll, in Catalonia, had reaffirmed its adherence to Roman and papal tradition by imitating Saint Peter's in the construction of its abbey church.

Roman art also persisted during the Carolingian period, through the continued use of mosaic decoration on the walls of churches and fidelity to the iconographic repertory of Late Antiquity. The late eighth century baptistery of Callixtus in Cividale, and the baldachin of Sant' Apollinare in Classe in Ravenna provide the best examples of the new uses to which Roman decoration was put.

Facing Italy on the other coast of the Mediterranean, Catalonia is a good example of autonomous regional development. There, architecture from the Carolingian period is known only through a few buildings which establish a link between the architecture of Late Antiquity and the pre-Romanesque forms that appeared during the second half of the tenth century. Here, too most paleo-Christian religious monuments continued in use till a late date.

Among the great surviving structures built before the tenth century are the three churches of Terrassa (Egara). On this site near Barcelona stand three monuments from an episcopal complex, dedicated respectively to Saint Peter, Saint Michael, and Saint Mary. They are composed of two Romanesque buildings built onto older chevets and a third structure contemporary with the chevets. The church of Santa María is formed of a large apse with a square exterior and horseshoe-arched interior; it was originally part of a basilica which seems likely to have had nave, flanking aisles, and transept.

San Miguel has a central plan, square on the outside and set off with four angled niches in the interior. It has been suggested that it served as a baptistery. For this reason, the architect J. Puig i Cadafalch, while restoring the structure, added a baptismal font crowned with a baldachin supported by eight columns and interesting capitals. To the east, a horseshoe-arched apse, its floor-level raised by the trilobed crypt on which it is built, presents a polygonal external plan on the exterior. The third basilica, San Pedro, has only a trilobed apse and a transept remaining from this period.

The three edifices of Terrassa, as they have just been described, are strictly contemporary and clearly distinguishable from earlier paleo-Christian as well as from later pre-Romanesque architecture. They probably date from the late ninth century, though this date is not unanimously accepted; some art historians adhere to the theory of J. Puig i Cadafalch and continue to date them to the Visigothic period. The masonry employed in this phase of construction of the Terrassa structures is of the classic Roman type, with small nearly aligned stone blocks alternating with rows of bricks.

The very large windows, the form of the apses, and the overall scale of the buildings lend them an air quite unlike that of other surviving Catalonian churches. They belong to a paleo-Christian tradition, as do the wall paintings that decorate the apses. In Catalonia, the horseshoe-arched apse with square or polygonal exterior predates the pre-Romanesque trapezoidal apse.

Other than the important group in Egara, extremely little is known of ninth-century religious architecture in this area. It probably employed methods of construction not very different from those of late Roman times, especially in the rural regions; walls composed of small blocks of uncut stone, joined at the angles with

The Visigothic architectural tradition in Carolingian Catalonia
San Miguel, Terrassa, exterior view from the southwest, end of the ninth–beginning of the tenth century. This edifice, built as a baptistery in the Visigothic period, forms a Greek cross, with at the east an apse richly ornamented with frescoes. Among the images is the Pantokrator, in a cruciform aureole carried by angels, surrounded perhaps by the twelve Apostles, each with his hand covering his mouth.

medium-size stones, supporting wooden roofs. Catalonia's situation on several major axes of communication and with an exposed coast left it frequently affected by wars and pillage, especially at the time of the Islamic raids, and the religious structures were therefore in a bad state of preservation by the end of the ninth century. A Carolingian document addressed to the bishop of Elne in 898 mentions that almost all of the churches in his diocese were falling into ruin and could no longer be restored. This state of affairs was confirmed the following year by an authorization from King Charles to the metropolitan of Narbonne.

This illustrates very clearly why so many restorations were necessary in rural areas during the Carolingian period. It was thanks to such campaigns of rebuilding that the new styles spread and became established throughout the empire during the course of the tenth century.

**Architectural balance
in a polyvalent space**
Axonometric projection of San
Miguel, Terrassa, end of the
ninth–beginning of the tenth
century. The edifice has a crypt,
perhaps a *martyrium,* under the
main apse.

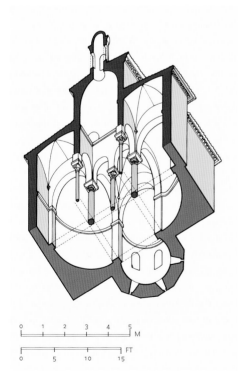

The Kingdom of Asturias

The Muslim invasion of 711 did not drive the Visigoths from the Iberian Peninsula. Following their victory over the Moors at Covadonga, they found themselves confined to a small part of of Asturias, situated between the mountains and the sea. During the reign of Alfonso I (739–757), the kingdom of the Asturias asserted its independence. He extended his kingdom's borders to the north of the peninsula. As the Moors retreated, Silo (774–778) established his capital at Pravia, where the basilica of Santiañez, consecrated to John the Evangelist, was built. The innovative plan for this edifice presented a double-bayed nave and aisles, a nonprojecting transept, and a chevet with three apses, each containing an altar. At Oviedo, to which the capital had been transferred prior to the accession of Alfonso II (791–842), the king had the city redesigned by the architect Tioda. Several churches rose up around the palace and the episcopal complex. The kings of Asturias paid particular attention to architecture in their capital and to their rural palatine residences.

The fierce desire of Alfonso I's successors, Fruela I and Alfonso II the Chaste, to fight the Muslims, and various difficulties experienced at Toledo, set the stage for the victory of Ordoño I at Clavijo (859) and furthered the reconquest of the peninsula. This project came closer to its goal with the establishment of the capital at Léon under Alfonso III the Great (866–910). Subsequently, the kingdom expanded toward the Duero valley and Galicia, where the ruler took steps to rebuild the basilica of Santiago de Compostela. Under Fruela II, about 924, the kingdom of Asturias became the kingdom of Asturias and Léon.

During the ninth century, the small kingdom of Asturias maintained systematic ties with the Carolingian Empire. The court art that developed there, which followed the Visigothic tradition, openly rejected all Islamic influence. Oviedo, the capital, was walled under Alfonso II. The royal palace was built at its center: a complex with private and public spaces, reception and ceremonial halls, and baths. At

The emergence of Christian Asturias
Map of the kingdom of Asturias, ninth century. The remaining supporters of the Visigothic monarchy settled in the region of Oviedo and in 718 created a Christian kingdom that provided shelter from the Muslims and established relations with the Carolingian Empire.

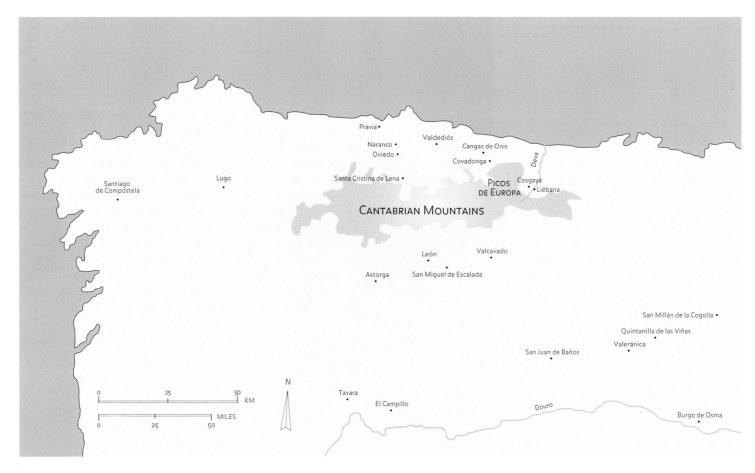

this time, the Cámara Santa was built, a mausoleum that housed the royal treasure, in which was placed the famous Cross of the Angels of the Kings of Oviedo, dating from 808. This structure reverted to the classic tradition of two-storey churches. Several churches were also built, including San Salvador and Santa María, on either side of the palace and San Tirso. The documentary sources emphasize the richness of San Tirso, which had a basilical plan with nave and flanking aisles; a rectangular east end survives.

The most important surviving monument of the period was built near the city of Oviedo between 812 and 842: San Julián de los Prados, or Santullano, a royal establishment. The church – 39 by 29 m – has nave and flanking aisles with three bays, a tripartite chevet with rectangular apses (each of which encloses an altar) a western porch, and two side porches placed at either end of the transept. The aisles are separated from the nave by large semicircular arcades resting on massive pillars. The remains of the wall paintings show decorative *trompe-l'œil* architecture that covered the entire wall surface; they are particularly well preserved in the transept.

Asturian religious architecture from the reign of Ramiro I (842–850) is known to us primarily through the surviving chapel of Santa Cristina de Lena, the palatine church of San Miguel de Lillo, perhaps built by the same architect, and the royal palace of Naranco.

The palace of Naranco is the most exceptional monument of the period. Located in the mountains not far from Oviedo, it is formed of large blocks of stone in the Visigothic tradition. The rectangular plan is that of the Cámara Santa of Oviedo, with two vaulted storeys. At each end of its short sides, the central rectangular space gives onto a gallery opening to the exterior through a triple arcade with

A rosary of palatine chapels
San Julián de los Prados, Santullano, Oviedo, exterior, end of the first third of the ninth century. It features a high, continuous transept, meollon masonry (roughly trimmed small stones) replacing the freestone favored in Spanish Visigothic architecture, and a return to the barrel vault, which here replaces the horseshoe arch.

Real and symbolic architectures
Detail of the painted decoration of San Julián de los Prados, Santullano, Oviedo, end of the first third of the ninth century. Above a plinth painted to resemble inlaid stones, the surviving decorative elements in the nave and transept consist of painted panels displaying pedimented palaces or churches below hangings.

Classical motifs
Detail of the painted decoration of San Julián de los Prados, Santullano, Oviedo, end of the first third of the ninth century. The painted decoration of the apses imitate coffers ornamented with various motifs. These wall paintings bear comparison with Roman illusionistic painting and its lineage in proto-Byzantine art.

The Visigothic tradition of compartmentalized space
San Julián de los Prados, Santullano, Oviedo, interior view of the nave from the transept, end of the first third of the ninth century. A high wall with an arch flanked by lateral arch-shaped openings treated as low windows, separates the body of the church from the transept, thus clearly delineating the elements of the edifice.

columns and Corinthian capitals. Inside, the first storey is a barrel-vaulted room whose transverse arches rest on dwarf walls. On the upper level transverse arches subtend the vault and blind arcades relieve the side walls with sculpted medallions in the spandrels. The reliefs and the sculpted capitals add to the richness of the decoration. On the exterior, buttresses shore up the structure. The four sides of the edifice each present a different façade. The main façade, on one of the long sides, has a double staircase giving access to the entry of the first floor; the rear façade was decorated with a balcony. The palace was turned into a church and consecrated to Saint Mary in 848, according to an inscription on the altar.

Dedicated to the archangel Michael, San Miguel de Lillo has a basilical plan and a chevet with three apses extending from the crossing of the projecting transept. Only a portion of the western façade remains, on the back of which there is, in true Carolingian fashion, a gallery. The sculpted decoration on the posts of the main door recalls the iconographical repertory of games and hunting of Late Antiquity, perhaps through the intermediary of consular diptychs (carvings presented by Roman consuls to those in power on assuming office).

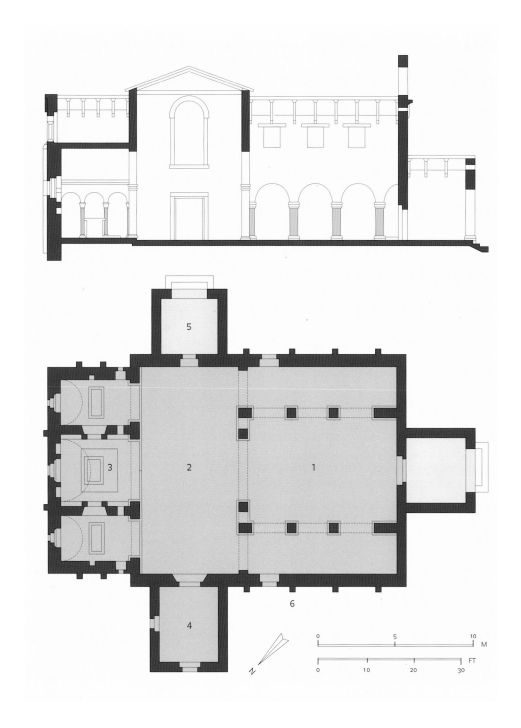

Integration of a high transept
with the nave and chevet
San Julián de los Prados,
Santullano, Oviedo, cross section
and plan, end of the first third of
the ninth century.
Above: Barrel vault, square pillars,
and rectangular openings.
Below: The high transept,
extended at the south by a
reconstructed porch and at the
north by a structure with galleries,
adjoins a tripartite chevet,
containing a room perhaps
intended for a hermit. Small
buttresses punctuate the external
walls.
1   Nave and aisles
2   Continuous high transept
3   Tripartite chevet
4   Structure with gallery
5   Porch
6   External buttresses

The third edifice of this group is the church of Santa Cristina at Polo de Lena. Here the architect has imitated the gallery on the reverse of the façade found at San Miguel de Lillo, while the elevation of the nave and the architectural decoration are similar to those of the palace of Naranco. Both San Salvador de Valdediós, consecrated in 893, and San Adrián de Tuñón, are of a later date.

Asturian architecture developed in a closed system with great continuity throughout the duration of the independent kingdom. The plans with nave and flanking aisles, tripartite chevets, and inner division of space are among its formal characteristics, together with the presence of a room high above the apses. Yet the third and last phase of Asturian architecture paved the way for new formulas destined to evolve during the Romanesque period.

The kingdom of Asturias, isolated in the north of the Iberian Peninsula, maintained close ties with the Carolingian world. The rest of the peninsula was Islamic, which gave ancient Roman "Hispania" a special role as a crucible of Oriental and Western culture. During the caliphate, Córdoba was a famous cultural, intellectual,

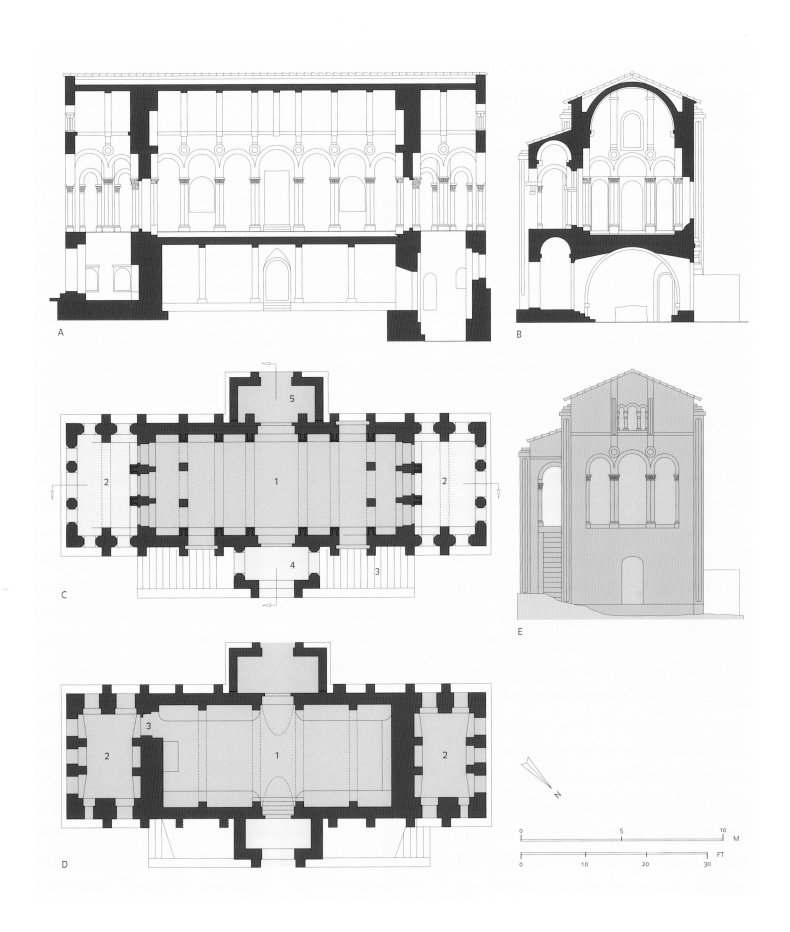

A two-storey palace

Palace-belvedere of Santa María de Naranco, Oviedo, containing an altar that was dedicated to the Virgin Mary on 24 June 848.

A Longitudinal section
B Vertical section
C Plan of the upper storey
  1 The barrel-vaulted main hall
  2 Three-arched side porches open to the exterior

3 Access stairways
4 Entrance porch
5 Balcony (now ruined)
D Plan of the ground floor
  1 Vaulted central room
  2 Timber-roofed side rooms

3 Door connecting the east side room with the main part of the structure
E West elevation

Architectural originality during the reign of Ramiro I
Santa María de Naranco, Oviedo, view of the eastern belvedere, mid-ninth century. The vaulted room elegantly opens onto the exterior by means of apertures on three sides consisting of stilted arches resting on the attached wreathed columns. The disks of the spandrels, ornamented with stylized animals, are connected to the brackets of the transverse arches by means of sculpted rectangular bands.

Page 203
Palatine architecture that dominates the landscape
Santa María de Naranco, Oviedo, exterior view of the palace-belvedere, mid-ninth century. A double staircase leads to the upper story, containing a single room ornamented with arcaded galleries. The freestone masonry is supported by buttresses in the form of engaged pilasters, which echo the attached columns within.

and scientific center whose influence spread to the north of the peninsula and, by way of Catalonia, to Europe.

Throughout the Middle Ages, until the reconquest reached Andalusia at the beginning of the Renaissance, the Iberian Peninsula remained at least partly Islamic territory. Especially in the early part of this period, the Mozarabs – Christians who continued to live in Islamic territory – contributed to cultural dialogue with the Christian territories, notably through the spread of architectural forms such as the horseshoe arch, and decorative elements in paintings, mosaics, and manuscripts.

The Christian reconquest of Spain involved the peninsula's northern kingdoms in a series of campaigns against the south, from the Early Middle Ages up to the Romanesque and Gothic periods. In the northern Christian kingdoms a Romanesque art appeared that evolved in close relation with the rest of Europe; its oldest expression, the first Romanesque art, is a masonry architecture found from Lombardy to Navarre during the first half of the eleventh century, and impacts a certain unity throughout southern Europe. The pre-Romanesque which had, during the tenth century, gradually taken over from Carolingian art, was its necessary antecedent.

The refinement of Asturian decoration
Detail of a capital from Santa María de Naranco, Oviedo, mid-ninth century. The wreathed column culminates in a braided astragal and a capital decorated with stylized flowers. Braiding, a major element in the decorative vocabulary of the Asturians, is beautifully illustrated here.

A highly compact architecture
San Miguel de Lillo, Oviedo, exterior, mid-ninth century. Only the west end of the church survives. This consists of a vaulted porch with galleries, flanked by two square side rooms, and a single bay of the high nave with aisles. The outside walls, re-inforced by buttresses, are pierced by unusual openings with geometric and rosette motifs.

Original treatment of a classical model
Decorative detail of one of the doorposts at the entrance of San Miguel de Lillo, Oviedo, mid-ninth century. This circus scene combines a lion tamer and an acrobat executing a flip. The upper register shows a consul opening the games. The work demonstrates the highly stylized nature and very low relief of Asturian sculpture.

Church of Santa Cristina de Lena,
Oviedo, mid-ninth century. A
vaulted rectangular-plan edifice
with low but deeply projecting
additions, composed of a porch,
an apsidal chapel, and two side
rooms. Once again, strong
buttresses are added to the
exterior shell.

Page 207
Architecture for a fixed liturgy
Church of Santa Cristina de Lena,
Oviedo, interior view of the choir,
mid-ninth century. Access to the
presbytery is gained by two side
stairways behind a cloister wall
comparable to an iconostasis,
formed by three arches that support slender colonnettes framing a
Visigothic chancel plaque. A
compartment-wall enclosing five
Visigothic lathice-work screens
rises over this group.

**A number of original
characteristics**
Church of Santa Cristina de Lena,
Oviedo, with a highly compartmentalized and complex structure,
mid-ninth century:

A Vertical section of the choir
   completed by a cloister wall
   comparable to an iconostasis
B Longitudinal section
   illustrating the complexity of
   the arrangement of the interior
   space
   1 Gallery of the porch
   2 Gallery of the vestibule and
     the west side of the nave
   3 Raised apse
C Plan showing the symmetrical
   arrangement of the edifice
   around its two axes
   1 Porch
   2 Vestibule and side rooms
   3 Central room
   4 Side rooms
   5 Cloister wall comparable to
     an iconostasis
   6 Apsidal chapel

**The royal patronage
of Alfonso III the Great**
San Salvador, Valdediós, exterior,
c. 893. The edifice contains a very
high nave with continuous barrel
vaulting, a tripartite chevet with a
mysterious small room above it,
as well as a galleried porch flanked
with two side rooms. The aisles
are reinforced by external
buttresses.

**Elegant openings and Moorish
inspiration**
Detail of the decoration of the
openings of the chevet of
San Salvador, Valdediós, c. 893.
The curve of the horseshoe arch
used for the arches of the
windows of the chevet, the gemel
windows of the nave, and the style
of their framing, suggest Muslim
influences overlaying the Asturian
sculptural tradition.

Pre-Romanesque palmettes

Detail of a capital from San Salvador, Valdediós, c. 893. The entrance arches of the apses and those of the triple-arcade windows lighting the chevet rest on columns that have capitals decorated with clumsily stylized foliage of distinctly "pre-Romanesque" appearance.

Pillary of a style pre-dating Ramiro I

San Salvador, Valdediós, interior view of the nave in the direction of the choir, c. 893. Aside from the ornate capitals, the large brick arcades of the nave are supported by massive pillars via capitals with only moulded decoration. This combination of decorative possibilities is typical of Asturian art.

The rules of Asturian architecture

San Salvador, Valdediós, built c. 893, sums up the Asturian style:
A Longitudinal section
  1 Porch with gallery
  2 Nave
  3 High room
B Vertical section
C Plan
  1 Open porch between two rooms
  2 Nave and aisles
  3 Rectangular annexes
  4 Tripartite chevet
  5 Portico of the southern aisle

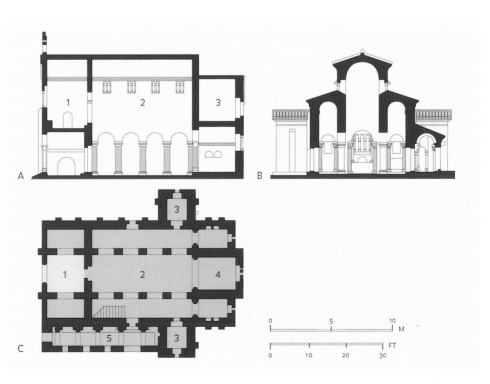

Mozarabic Architecture

The Mozarabs lived mainly in the large cities, such as Córdoba (the seat of the caliphate), Toledo, and Granada. Until the early ninth century, the Mozarabs enjoyed freedom of worship in return for a modest tax. Thereafter, following a number of uprisings, they lost their rights and began to move into the liberated northern areas, such as Asturias, León, and Galicia. This important immigration has often been evoked to explain the presence of Moorish-influenced architectural elements, such as "chisel-curl" brackets or the horseshoe arch, in the north of the Iberian Peninsula. True, the horseshoe arch had already appeared in paleo-Christian architecture, in Ravenna, for example, in Roman architecture, and, later, in Visigothic Spain; but the Islamic horseshoe arch was more closed at the span and presented a narrower space between the piers in comparison with the Roman horseshoe arch, whose springers projected.

The term "Mozarabic" has often, mistakenly, been used to designate Hispanic Christian art of Islamic influence, but should be used more narrowly. Mozarabic architecture has even been called the architecture of the Reconquest or Repopulation. Its character was determined by two influences; that of the Hispanic liturgy, shown in the division of internal spaces, and that of Andalusian Muslim art, seen in the use of the horseshoe arch as well as very narrow apses and certain decorative details. So-called Mozarabic edifices follow the basilical plan or a special plan that combines the basilical with the cruciform plan of Visigothic tradition. The interior space is highly compartmented, composed of small, quadrangular spaces with chancels or low walls that separate the apses and the transept.

Bobastro, in the Ronda hills near Málaga, possesses the only church that can be

Islamic art and the Visigothic heritage
San Miguel de la Escalada, León, exterior, c. 913. This edifice built from very large stones is enlivened by bands of chevron decoration like gear teeth and the large, lobed modillions of the roof. This sturdy appearance, reinforced by a freestone tower built after Alfonso VII granted the monastery to the canons of Saint-Ruf of Avignon in 1155, is somewhat softened by the elegance of the Mozarabic arcade.

A Mozarabic symbol
San Miguel de la Escalada, León, exterior view of the southern arcade, c. 913. The arcade opens to the outside by means of a series of twelve horseshoe arches on columns with Corinthian capitals. In the remainder of the church, two other decorative systems are found; one is based on re-used Corinthian capitals, the other, found on friezes, in the apses and in the chancels, on flowers, palmettes, shells, and various animal motifs.

attributed to Mozarabs living with the Muslim enclave. If we take account of the fact that the Muslim leader Omar Ben Hafsun, who was born to Christian parents, withdrew to this area after his conversion to Christianity in 899, we may perhaps date the church to its early tenth century (899–917). Carved from the living rock, this church has a basilical plan with nave flanked by aisles, and the compartmented transept is separated from the apses by a low wall. The apses are unequal in size, and the central apse is horseshoe-shaped.

San Miguel de la Escalada is falsely considered Mozarabic. It stands in the Kingdom of León and was completed in 913. The aisles, like the higher and broader nave, are timber-roofed, and lead through the crossing to three horseshoe-plan apses. These are separated from the transept by a chancel. A covered gallery to the south, which serves as a porch, possesses a series of horseshoe arches that are among the most beautiful of the period. This monument's originality and quality derive from its sculpture, especially the various series of sculpted capitals. These are a feature of the columns that divide the interior spaces and those of the porch; they constitute a reinterpretation of the Corinthian order, while the final series provides an effect comparable to friezes.

Near Valladolid, the church of San Cebrián de Mazote is of the same type as San Miguel. Timber-roofed, it has a nave flanked by aisles and a transept with rounded arms. The whole is trilobed in form. In the chevet, the main apse is flanked by two rectangular groin-vaulted chapels. A counterapse has been placed at the east, thus creating another sanctuary. This monument's horseshoe arches also number among the most beautiful of the period. The church was one source of new interpretations of the architectural orders that later found a measure of success.

Decorative motifs
Detail of an aedicule of
San Miguel de la Escalada, León,
c. 913. This window at the west
end of the portico has horseshoe
arches and a raised rectangular
frame characteristic of Mozarabic
decoration.

The Arabic aesthetic of Córdoba
San Miguel de la Escalada, León,
interior, c. 913. The interior space,
organized by the horseshoe arch,
is characterized by a very airy
spatial division created by
columns adorned with capitals.
This rather fragile support made
a timber roof necessary; the roof
is supported by the walls of the
arcades, illuminated by high
windows.

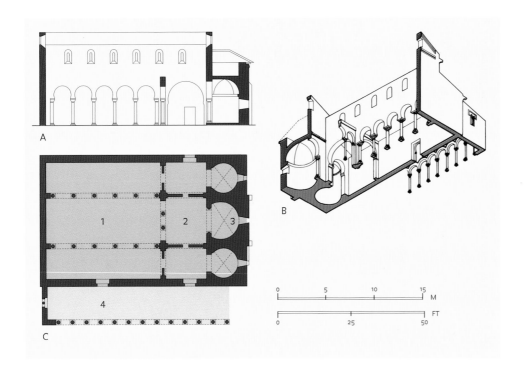

Horseshoe-shaped apses
in a rectangular mass
San Miguel de la Escalada, León,
c. 913:
A Cross section
B Axonometric projection
C Plan
   1 Nave with single-storey
     aisles and direct lighting
   2 Transept separated from the
     main space by a triple
     ornamental arcade
   3 Tripartite chevet with
     horseshoe-shaped apse and
     absidioles set in a solid
     rectangular mass
   4 Side portico

The presence of a relief depicting two figures facing one another is the more remarkable in that most "Mozarabic" religious buildings in Castile or León have no figural sculpted decoration. The Muslim influence has been invoked in explanation of this; there are no images in Islamic art. On the other hand, Mozarabic architecture is very rich in decorative sculpture, numerous geometric and plant motifs (fleurons, scrolls, frets, and palmettes) cover not only capitals but friezes, pilasters, and chancels.

Churches such as Santa María de Lebeña (built in 924) and Santa María de Wamba demonstrate strong similarities between "Mozarabic" and Asturian architecture and, through Asturian, with Visigothic architecture. The church of Santiago de .Peñalba, in the region of León, dates from the second quarter of the tenth century. It has a nave without aisles and a projecting transept. The eastern apse is almost identical to the western one. The crossing is surmounted by a dome, a popular architectural element of the period, forming a shape like a small tower on the exterior. The oratory of San Miguel de Celanova near Orense, founded in 936, also has a nave without aisles. The upper church of San Millán de Suso in Old Castile, in the monastery of San Millán de la Cogolla in Logroño, was built in the final years of the tenth century in memory of the first hermits who settled in the place. Finally, the hermitage of San Baudelio de Berlanga, near Soria, probably dates from the early eleventh century. It is of quadrangular plan with a central column; the vaulting is supported by eight radial horseshoe arches. A gallery built into the choir forms an enclosed space that was used as an oratory.

During the "Mozarabic" period, that is, the Hispanic Early Middle Ages, the Beatus manuscripts first emerged. They owe their name to the eighth-century commentaries of Beatus, the abbot of Liébana (Asturias), on the Books of Daniel and the Apocalypse. Many are illustrated and were often copied at the courts during the tenth century, and even later. The illustrations derive from Visigothic, Islamic, and even Carolingian influences. Among the most notable Beatus manuscripts are the one in the collection of the Pierpont Morgan Library, New York; the Tábara Beatus (Archivo Histórico Nacional, Madrid); the one belonging to the cathedral of León; and, finally, the Apocalypse of the Museu de la Catedral de Girona. Their great originality lies in their treatment of the human figure and use of extremely bright colors.

The Visigothic tradition defined in volumes and exterior decoration
Santa María de Lebeña, exterior, c. 924. The narrow high nave, grafted onto a choir divided into three rectangular chapels, is extended by a room with two annexes communicating with the aisles. All these elements derive from the Asturian tradition, as do the lobed modillions of the roofs ornamented with friezes, stylized foliage scrollwork, and stars.

"Mozarabic" art
Santa María de Lebeña, interior, c. 924. The nave, the three west compartments of the church and the three apses have barrel vaults running lengthwise, while those of the aisles run crosswise. Typical of the "Mozarabic" style are the horseshoe arches and the capitals with their Corinthian-derived decoration.

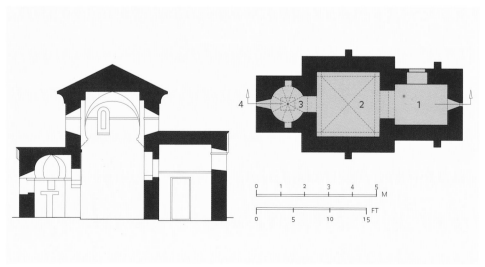

Three spaces in a row
San Miguel de Celanova, Galicia, cross section and plan, c. 936. This chapel contains three square compartments: a choir, as sturdy in plan as in elevation, a small barrel-vaulted nave, and a rib-vaulted apse.

1 Nave
2 Groin-vaulted choir
3 Apse
4 Keyhole window

Page 216 above
The Visigothic tradition
San Miguel de Celanova, Galicia, exterior, c. 936. The structure of this chapel, composed of large blocks of granite, recalls Visigothic technique, the effect is reinforced by the treatment of the enormous chisel-curl modillions, supporting the broad eaves of the choir roof.

The horseshoe arch, distinguishing feature of Mozarabic art
Church of San Millán de la Cogolla, with its colonnade separating the constructed part from the rock-cut nave.

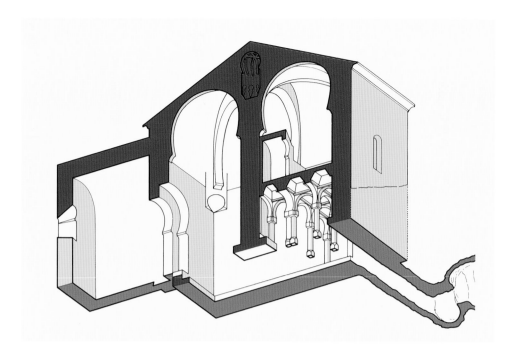

**The gallery that divides
the internal space**
Axonometric projection of the
hermitage of San Baudelio de
Berlanga, León, c. 913. Beneath
the building is an underground
gallery. A hidden opening leads
to a cave.

Below
Entirely painted edifice
San Baudelio contains a nave with
gallery and a square apse. The
central pillar supports the
diagonal and axial arches and
carries at its top a small loggia
pierced with horseshoe-shaped
openings and covered
with a ribbed vault.

delignouiae quod ega Inparadisodi mī
Explicithistoria

NCIPITEXPLANATIOSVPRASCRIPTE
Istorie Inliprosecvndo
Angeloefferiecclesie scribe
Subuniusappellacioneangeli omniū

Page 219
A central pillar in the form of a palm tree
San Baudelio de Berlanga, León, interior view of the central part of the nave, c. 913. A stairway gives access to the gallery. The umbrella vault, carried by eight square-section horseshoe-shaped ribs radiating from a central pillar, produces a distinctly original effect.

Above
Mozarabic miniatures favor apocalyptic themes
The "Beatus of El Escorial", second half of the tenth century. The church of Smyrna is represented by an abstract shape: a square border decorated with geometric motifs. It serves as a frame somewhat monumental figures of the actors. John delivers the Divine message to one of the angels of the seven churches. (Biblioteca del Monasterio de San Lorenzo, El Escorial)

Below
Ideal and unnaturalistic architectures
Beatus of Girona, Catalonia, 975. Here the actors are dominated by the high structures crowned by towers and featuring an iconostasis of horseshoe arches with curtains tied open. In the background, these give way to apses with T-shaped altars. The Divine message from John is delivered to one of the angels of the seven churches. (Museo diocesano, Girona)

Page 221
Schematic outlines in vivid colours
Beatus of Facundus, end of the tenth century. A distinctive feature of the codex is its background of horizontal bands in intense colors. The treatment of the human figure is equally individual. "They worshipped the beast and the dragon." (Biblioteca nacional, Madrid)

UBI ROGES TERRE
BESTIA & DRACONE
ADORANT.

HEC BESTIA
ASCENDIT DE
ABISSO.

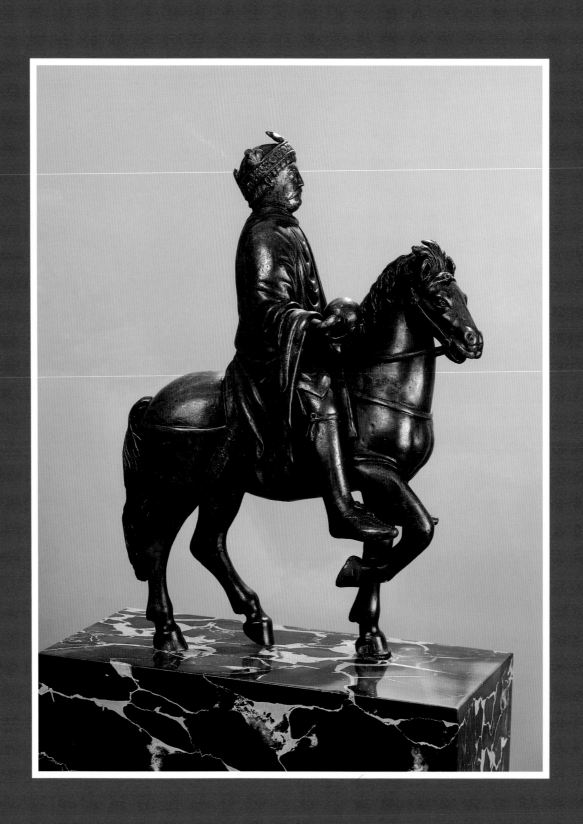

CONCLUSION

The Carolingian Heritage

From the episcopal complex at Metz to Centula/Saint-Riquier, passing through the Palatine Chapel at Aachen, the ideal abbey church in the plan of St. Gall, and the cathedral of Cologne, Carolingian architecture was an elaboration of the models that transmitted the heritage and prestige of Late Antiquity to the Middle Ages. At Saint-Bénigne in Dijon, for example, the classical-inspired Sainte-Marie rotunda represented the culminating point of the the development of the Carolingian chevet in Burgundy.

The growth of the cult of relics, the increasing size of sanctuaries, and the multiplication of altars gave rise to the magnificent goldwork of the Carolingian period; its altar frontals, reliquary statues, and book covers played an important role in the development of later monumental sculpture.

The relationship between monumental architecture and the production of church furnishings and decorative objects was very close in the Carolingian period. A particularly eloquent example is provided by the reliquary in the form of a triumphal arch offered by Einhard to Sint Servaas in Maastricht in 828. The object is known to us through an old drawing in the Bibliothèque Nationale in Paris. It probably served as the base of a cross; its rich decoration derives from Roman and paleo-Christian triumphal designs and foreshadows the monumental iconography deployed in the great Romanesque portals. An analogous monumentality is found in the bronze statuette, said to be of Charlemagne, in the collection of the Musée du Louvre; it expresses the essence of the Carolingian aesthetic, torn between a nostalgia for Antiquity and the creation of a medieval language.

In the tenth century, that tension was no longer so acute, though the overall continuity between Antiquity and the Middle Ages was not interrupted. Church choirs grew ever richer, with decorated liturgical furnishings further enhancing the status of the altar. The development of the absidial ambulatory, with the addition, in the cathedrals of Clermont-Ferrand and Thérouanne, of radiating chapels, could be a final stage in the trend to accentuate the importance of the east end.

In comparison with the Carolingian period, a marked feature of the tenth century was the creation of regional styles. From the late ninth century, numerous Carolingian documents relating, for example, to the south of France, mention the condition of certain edifices and the problems involved in restoring them, particularly in rural areas. A great tide of reconstruction followed. Confining ourselves to the borders of present-day France, we note the passage from the use of earth mortar to one of limestone and gravel, and the sheer scale of the new reconstructed buildings; the abbey church of Saint-Michel de Cuxa and Adalbero's Reims Cathedral are two very different but highly eloquent examples of this process.

Carolingian art was marked by the strong personality of Charlemagne and the profound involvement of his court in artistic creation. The art of the tenth century was more diversified and fragmental. Yet the dream of imperial grandeur and unity of the Carolingians was, as we shall see, of lasting architectural influence.

With the advent of the Capetians, signaled by the coronation of Hugues Capet

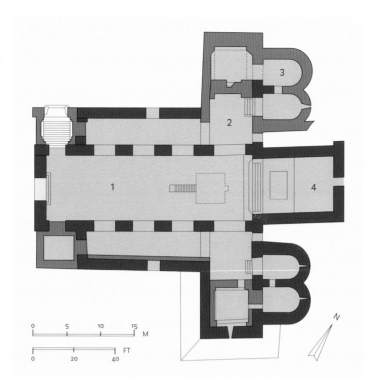

The architecture of the late tenth century in southern France
Saint-Michel de Cuxa, plan of the pre-Romanesque building, 956–974. The nave leads to a rectangular apse. It and the aisles communicate, via horseshoe arches with a projecting transept endowed with four oblong absidioles. The two absidioles on each side are contiguous and covered by horseshoe-shaped barrel vaults.
1 Nave with aisles
2 Projecting transept
3 Deep absidioles
4 Rectangular apse originally opening onto the transept via an arcade of horseshoe arches

Page 225
Simplicity of forms and volumes
Abbey church of Saint-Michel de Cuxa, interior view of the nave, second half of the tenth century. The nave opens onto the aisles via three large arches.

An annular vault from the end of the first millenium
Saint-Michel de Cuxa, interior view of the crypt of the Virgin of the Nativity. This chapel, built for the veneration of relics of the Nativity, is covered with a semicircular annular vault rising from a central pillar. Ventilation via three loopholes has helped to conserve pieces of wood from the centering of the vault, which became embedded in the eleventh century lime motar.

as king of the Franks in 987 by Adalbero in Reims, the West emerged from a period of insecurity brought about by successive waves of migratory peoples. The millenium was approaching. Radulfus Glaber, a Cluniac monk and the historian of his time, left us a famous account of the reconstruction movement that transformed church architecture throughout the West. His conclusion is a fitting conclusion to this volume. As he put it, "The Christian nations vied for the glory of the most remarkable temple".

CHRONOLOGICAL TABLE

Saint-Peter's on the Vatican:
Constantinian basilica, Rome

Mausoleum of Santa Costanza,
Rome

Monuments

308–319	Aquileia: church of Theodore
312–315	Rome: arch of Constantine
320–340	Vatican: church of Saint Peter's, founded by Constantine I
after 326	Rome: Episcopal Church and baptistery of San Giovanni in Laterano by Constantine I
c. 382	Milan: basilica Apostolorum
384–399	Rome: church of Santa Pudenziana, founded by Pope Siricius
386	Rome: San Paolo fuori le Mura

c. 418	Marseilles: monastery of Saint-Victor
c. 425	Ravenna: San Giovanni Evangelista
432	Rome: reconstruction of Santa Maria Maggiore and the baptistery of San Giovanni in Laterano
c. 450	Ravenna: Tomb of Galla Placidia
	Ravenna: baptistery of the Orthodox
	Clermont-Ferrand: cathedral
	Toulouse: Notre-Dame-de-la-Daurade
460–491	Tours: basilica of Saint-Martin
c. 475	Vienne: basilica des Apôtres
490–520	Ravenna: Arian Baptistery
c. 491	Auxerre: basilica of Saint-Germain
End 5th–early 6th century	
	Vienne: basilica of Saint-Pierre

4th century A.D.   5th century A.D.

Historical Events

Dome of the Arian Baptistery, Ravenna

312	Victory of Constantine I over Maxentius
314	Council of Arles
324	Victory of Constantine I over Licinius
306–337	Constantine I, emperor
325	First Council of Nicaea
337–361	Reign of Constantine II
352–366	Pontificate of Liberius
361–363	Reign of Julian
366–384	Pontificate of Damasus I
374–397	Saint Ambrose, Bishop of Milan
379–395	Reign of Theodosius
395–423	Reign of Honorius I, Roman Emperor of the West

400	First Council of Toledo
402–476	Ravenna is capital of the Western Empire
406–407	The Sueves and Vandals invade Gaul
408	Alaric returns to Italy
409	The Sueves and Vandals invade Spain
410	Alaric invades Rome
415	Athanulf assassinated
432–440	Pontificate of Sixtus III
440–461	Pontificate of Leo the Great
451–452	Attila is in Gaul, then Italy is defeated at the Battle of the Catalaunian Plains
455	Rome taken by the Vandals
476	End of the Western Roman Empire
481–511	Reign of Clovis
488–493	Theodoric the Great in Italy
493	Victory of Theodoric the Great over Odoacer

Paleo-Christian painting from the
Cemetery of Commodilla, Rome

Sant'Apollinare Nuovo, Ravenna

507 Paris: basilica des Apôtres
c. 520 Ravenna: completion of Sant'Apollinare Nuovo
before 526 Ravenna: mausoleum of Theodoric the Great
521–547 Ravenna: basilica of San Vitale
549 Ravenna: consecration of the basilica of Sant'Apollinare in Classe
552–557 Metz: enlargement of the cathedral of Saint-Étienne
c. 555 Poitiers: founding of the monastery of Sainte-Croix
c. 558 Nantes: cathedral
c. 570 Toulouse: basilica of Saint-Sernin
589–600 Autun: founding of the monastery of Saint-Martin
590 Luxeuil: founding of the monastery
End 6th century
Rome: crypt of the basilica of Saint Peter's

c. 609 Consecration of the pantheon to the Virgin by Pope Boniface IV
612 Founding of the monastery of Bobbio
613 Founding of the monastery of St. Gall
c. 630–680 Founding of the abbey of Jouarre
635 Northumbria: founding of the convent of Lindisfarne
c. 650 Founding of the abbey of Fontanella
c. 650–700 Santa María de Quintanilla de las Viñas
654 Jumièges: founding of the abbey
661 Asturias: consecration of the church of San Juan de Baños
after 673 Funerary crypt of the abbey of Jouarre
674 Founding of the monastery of Monkwearmouth
698 Founding of the abbey of Echternach

Beginning 8th century
Poitiers: *hypogeum* of Dunes
724 Founding of the monastery of Reichenau
c. 737 Cividale: baptistery of Calixtus
c. 750 Fulda: abbey of Saint-Denis
752–757 Rome: belfry tower of the basilica of Saint Peter's

6th century A.D.

507 Victory of Clovis at Vouillé
509–531 The Visigoths in Spain
510 Publication of the Salic Law
527–565 Reign of Justinian
after 534 Drawing up of the Rule of Saint Benedict
537 Siege of Rome by the Goths
540 Ravenna captured by the Byzantines
541–542 Childeric campaigns against the Visigoths in Spain
546 Rome captured by the Ostrogoths
553 The Franks and Alemanni in northern Italy
560 The Visigothic court in Toledo
568 The Lombards invade northern Italy
573–584 Episcopate of Gregory of Tours
584 The beginning of the struggle against the Lombards in Ravenna
587 Visigothic king Rekhared converts to Catholicism
590–604 Pontificate of Gregory I the Great

7th century A.D.

617 England ruled by Edwin, King of Northumbria
627 Conversion of King Edwin
629 Expulsion of the Byzantines from Spain by Swinthila
629–639 Reign of Dagobert I in Gaul
633 4th Council of Toledo, presided over by Isidore of Seville
636 Death of Isidore of Seville
653 Conversion of the Lombards to Christianity
663–664 Synod of Whitby: Rome's authority imposed on the Britons
668–670 Imposition of the Roman rites by Theodore of Tarsus, future Archbishop of Canterbury
672–735 the Venerable Bede's *Historia ecclesiastica gentis Anglorum*
673–677 Siege of Constantinople
675 Assassination of Childerich
680 Pépin of Herstal, mayor of the palace of Austrasia
687 Death of Cuthbert, Bishop of Lindisfarne

Tomb of Galla Placidia, Ravenna

8th century A.D.

711–713 Conquest of Spain by the Arabs
716–754 Saint Boniface's missionary work in Germany results in the foundation of the German Church
722 Reconquest of the Iberian Peninsula begins from Asturias
731 Pope Gregory III condemns iconoclasm
732–735 Charles Martel drives the Arabs from Gaul and takes control of Aquitaine
739 Lombards capture Rome
739–757 Alfonso I rules Asturias
743–751 Reign of Childerich III, the last Merovingian
751 Ravenna captured by the Lombards

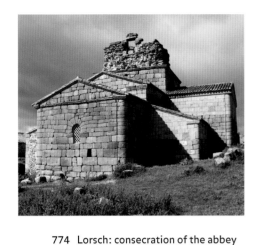

Santa María de Melque, Toledo

774 Lorsch: consecration of the abbey
774–787 Ingelheim: Carolingian palace
775 Saint-Denis: consecration of the abbey church of Saint-Denis
after 777 Nijmegen: Carolingian palace
779–780 Corvey, founding of the abbey
790–799 Centula: reconstruction of the abbey of Saint-Riquier
790–819 Fulda: enlargement of the church
c. 792 Aachen: construction of the palace by Odo of Metz

799 Nijmegen: consecration of the church of the palace
Saint-Riquier: consecration of the abbey church
799–814 Lyons: reconstruction of the church des Saints-Apôtres
799–816 Reichenau: reconstruction of the abbey church
799–after 816
Lyons: cathedral of Saint-Jean
799–818 Germigny-des-Prés: villa and oratory of Theodulf
End 8th century
Agaune: basilica of Saint-Maurice

800–850 Paderborn: Blessed Savior II
c. 800 Founding of the abbeys of Caunes, Cruas, Mondelieu, and Saint-Savin-sur-Gartempe
Cologne: new cathedral
804 Gellone: founding of the Abbey
805 Dalmatia: consecration of Saint Donat in Zadar
814–819 Noirmoutier: first church of Saint-Philibert-de-Grandlieu
814 Founding of the Abbey of Cornelimunster
814–826 Church of St.-Quentin
816 Brescia: San Salvatore
Corvey: founding of the Abbey
816–817 Plan of St. Gall
816–836 Reims: Sainte-Marie
816–841 Soissons: crypts of Saint-Médard
816–862 Reims: cathedral
817 Inden: consecration of the Abbey church

8th century A.D.

8th century A.D.

9th century A.D.

756 Siege of Rome by Aistulf
Pépin's Italian expedition
761–771 Iconoclastic controversy
768 Subjection of Aquitaine
Division of the kingdom between Charles and Carloman, Kings of the Franks
771 Death of Carloman; Charlemagne becomes sole King
772–774 Desiderius invades the Papal States
Siege of Pavia by Charlemagne, king of the Lombards
778 Charlemagne in Spain
785 Conquest of Saxony
786 Imposition of the Roman liturgy by Charlemagne

c. 791 First Norman invasions of Great Britain
795–816 Pontificate of Leo III
796–804 Alcuin is abbot of Saint-Martin in Tours
798–821 Theodulf, abbot of Saint-Benoît-sur-Loire and bishop of Orléans

800 Coronation of Charlemagne in Rome
De Villis Capitulary
801 Dalmatian Expedition
803 Capture of Barcelona
805–806 Conquest of Bohemia
807 Harun al-Rashid recognizes the rights of the Franks in the Holy Lands of Palestine
809–812 Conquest of Venetia
Spanish March created
810 Sack of Friesland by the Danes
814 Death of Charlemagne
816 Coronation of Louis the Pious in Reims
817 Einhard is Lothair's tutor
817–824 Pontificate of Paschal I
820 Presence of the Normans at the mouth of the Seine
823 Coronation of Lothair
823–855 Drogon is Bishop of Metz
827–844 Pontificate of Gregory IV

Palatine Chapel of Charlemagne, Aachen

817–824 Rome: chapel of San Zeno at Santa Prassede

817–824 Seligenstadt: church

820–822 Fulda: church of St. Michael

c. 820 Construction of the Church at the Abbey of Charroux

822–844 Corvey: first church

823–833 Fontanella: reconstruction of the abbey

824–857 Auxerre: restoration of the cathedrals Saint-Étienne and Notre-Dame
Reconstruction of the baptistery

827 Steinbach: consecration of the abbey

before 828 Monastery of Schänis

c. 830 Noirmoutier: fortification of the monastery

831–832 Limoges: consecration of the church of Saint-Sauveur-et-Saint-Martial

Santa María de Quintanilla de las Viñas

832 Saint-Denis: consecration of the chapel erected in the chevet

833–835 Le Mans: cathedral

836 Koblenz: consecration of the church of Saint Castor

836–846 Noirmoutier: enlargement of Saint-Philibert-de-Grandlieu

841–859 Auxerre: crypts of Saint-Germain

842–850 Asturias: Palace of Naranco
San Miguel de Lillo
Santa Cristina de Pola de Lena

c. 846 Saint-Omer: fortifications

847–855 Rome: Repair of San Paolo fuori le Mura and of Saint Peter's

852 Reims: consecration of Saint-Rémi

852–876 Hildesheim: cathedral

855 Fortification of the monastery of St. Gall

859 Halberstadt: consecration of the cathedral

860–867 Corvey: new chevet

862 Reims: consecration of the second cathedral

862–875 Construction of the church and crypt of the monastery of Maxence

863–875 Heiligenberg: church of Sankt Michael

864–878 Crypts of Saint-Pierre at Flavigny

869 Reconstruction of the city walls in Mans, Tours, and Dijon

871–880 Dijon: reconstruction of the church of Saint-Bénigne

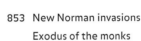

9th century A.D.

9th century A.D.

9th century A.D.

830 Rebellion of Lothair and his brothers

831 Louis the Pious regains power

838 Coronation of Charles the Bald
Death of Pépin
Sack of Marseilles by the Saracens

840 Deaths of Louis the Pious and Einhard
Beginning of the major invasions of England by the Normans

843–877 Reign of Charles the Bald

841 The Normans attack Quentovic
Destruction of Jumièges

843 Treaty of Verdun
Sack of Nantes by the Normans
Destruction of the abbey of Indret
Exodus of the monks of Vertou

845 Destruction of Centula and the basilica Sainte-Geneviève in Paris by the Normans

847–855 Pontificate of Leo IV

849–850 Saracen raids in Provence

853 New Norman invasions
Exodus of the monks
Transfer of the relics

855 Deaths of Lothair I and Leo IV

856 Sack of Orléans by the Normans
Entry into Paris

857 Assassination of Frotbald, Bishop of Chartres, by the Normans

858–867 Pontificate of Nicholas I

859–860 Norman raids around Spain

862 Death of Lupus, Abbot of Ferrières
Cyril and Methodius in Moravia

863 Sack of Poitiers by the Normans

863–864 Charles the Bald in Aquitaine
Presence of the Normans in Clermont
Assembly at Pitres

865 Sack of Saint-Benoît-sur-Loire

866 Death of Robert the Strong

867–872 Pontificate of Hadrian II

869 Death of Lothair II
Assassination of the Bishop of Orléans by the Saracens

872 Presence of the Normans in Angers

872–882 Pontificate of John VIII

875 Coronation of Charles the Bald in Rome
Invasion of France by Louis the German

876 Coronation of Charles II, King of Italy
Death of Louis the German
Norman invasion of the Seine Valley

877 Capitulation of Quierzy
Death of Charles the Bald

877–879 Reign of Louis II the Stammerer

878 Coronation of Carloman as King of Italy
Pope requests help from France against the Hungarians

Saint-Laurent, Grenoble

Sankt Michael, Hildesheim

873–885 Corvey: church and abbey
c. 878 Compiègne: fortifications
Flavigny: consecration of the abbey church
c. 879 Milan: oratory of San Satiro
c. 885 Autun: restoration of the abbey church of Saint-Martin
888–913 Reichenau-Oberzell: church of Sankt Georg
889–890 Fortification of the monasteries of Vézelay, Tournus, and Corbie
897–910 Nantes: reconstruction and fortification of the cathedral

Early 10th century
Terrassa: episcopal group
910 Souillac: founding of the abbey
913–952 Minden: carolingian cathedral
920–940 Sens: enlargement of the crypts of the church of Saint-Pierre-le-Vif
933–961 Auxerre: enlargement of the choir of the cathedral of Saint-Étienne
c. 934 Jumièges: hasty restoration of the ruins
before 936 Quedlinburg: crypt of Saint Wipert
937–948 Fulda: addition of two high, round towers to the secondary chevet of the abbey church
938 Tours: fortification of the church of Saint-Martin
before 943 Werden/Ruhr: construction of the westwork of the abbey church of the Holy Savior
946 Clermont-Ferrand: consecration of the cathedral of Notre-Dame

960–979 Tournus: construction of the second abbey church of Saint-Philibert
963–981 Cluny: construction of the second abbey church by Abbot Mayeul
965 Cologne: reconstruction of the church of Sankt Maria im Kapitol
972–1008 Liège: construction of Saint-Jean
975–1009 Mainz: construction of the cathedral
976 Reims: construction of the porch–bell tower of the cathedral
980 Cologne: consecration of the abbey church of Sankt Pantaleon
980–990 Jumièges: construction of Saint-Pierre
984 Metz: reconstruction of the cathedral begins
989–1029 Orléans: construction of the church of Saint-Aignan
996 Hildesheim: founding of the abbey of Sankt Michael
before 998 Beauvais: church of Notre-Dame de la Basse-Œuvre

9th century A. D.

10th century A. D.

10th century A. D.

879–882 Death of Louis the Stammerer
Reigns of Louis III and Carloman
Presence of the Normans in Ghent
881 Anoiating of Charles the Fat
New Norman invasions
Transfer of the treasure of Aachen to Stavelot
882–885 Presence of the Normans in the Rhineland
Defeat of the Normans
884 Death of Carloman
Coronation of Charles the Fat
885–886 Siege of Paris by the Normans
885–891 Pontificate of Stephen V
886 Destruction of the monasteries of Saint-Germain in Auxerre, Bèze, Dijon, and Flavigny
Bishop of Nantes flees to Angers
887 Charles III the Fat deposed
Election of Odo as king
888 Normans routed at Montfaucon by Odo
890–972 Saracens occupy La Garde-Freinet in the Var
892–923 Reign of Charles III the Simple
897 Assassination of Pope Stephen VI

900 Episcopal seat transferred from Iria Flavia to Santiago de Compostela
902 Victory of Alfonso III the Great at Zamora
909 Arabic conquest of Sicily completed
910 Founding of the abbey of Cluny by William I of Aquitaine
911 Conrad I elected King of Germany
913 León becomes capital of Asturias
914–928 Pontificate of John X
918 The Hungarians invade the Rhone valley, Lorraine, and Champagne
924 Death of Conrad I of Germany
929 Beginning of the Caliphate of Córdoba
930–937 Hungarians raid Burgundy
936 Otto I, King of Germany
936–954 Louis IV d'Outremer, King of France
940 Lorraine rejoins to the Empire
948–994 Mayeul, Abbot of Cluny
951 Otto I, King of Lombardy
954–986 Reign of Lothair, son of Louis IV, in France
955 Battle of Lechfeld: Otto I defeats the Hungarians

962 Otto I is crowned Roman Emperor by Pope John XII
966 Mieszko I, King of Poland, is baptized
Founding of the Christian Polish state
973 Death of Otto I
973–983 Reign of Otto II
977–993 Episcopate of Egbert of Trier
977–1002 Al-Mansur attempts Arabic reconquest of Spain
985 Sack of Barcelona by al-Mansur
987–996 Hugh Capet is proclaimed King of France at Noyon
Founding of the Capetian dynasty
987 Baptism of Vladimir, grand duke of Kiev
990–1031 William of Volpiano is Abbot of Saint-Bénigne in Dijon
994–1049 Odilon is Abbot of Cluny
996–1031 Robert the Pious is King of France
997 Destruction of the basilica of Santiago de Compostela by al-Mansur
999–1003 Pontificate of Sylvester II

Glossary

Abbey: community of monks or nuns led by an abbot or abbess.

Absidiole: small apse grafted onto the ambulatory, the transept, or the aisles of a church.

Aisle: one of the secondary naves that flank the central nave of a church.

Ambo: pulpit or chair in stone, often raised above the floor of the church, located in front of the choir or in the nave.

Ambulatory: encircling semicircular gallery placed at the extension of the aisles that encompasses the choir in a church.

Apse: from the Greek *hapsis* and the Latin *absis* or *apsis,* circle, vault. Semicircular or polygonal interior space that opens on the structure's open central space or a room.

Arcade: open bay covered by an arch supported by pillars or columns.

Arch: architectural element that connects two supports separated by a space. The round arch offers a semicircular profile; the stilted arch is higher than it is wide; the segmental arch wider than it is high; the lancet arch is composed of two segments of circles that intersect, forming a point; in the horseshoe arch, the curve continues beyond the semicircle; the ogee arch has two identical facing curves, each composed of two arcs, successively concave and convex; the trefoil arch is made by the juxtaposition of many segments of a circle.

Architrave: lowest part of an entablature, that rests directly on the capitals of columns or on other vertical supports.

Arianism: Christian heresy originating from the doctrine of Arius, a priest living in Alex-andria (c. 320) who acknow-ledged the fullness and divinity of only the Father in the Trinity. It was condemned by the Council of Nicaea in 325 and by the Council of Constantinople in 381.

Atrium: in paleo-Christian architecture, a court surrounded by porticoes on at least three sides, generally placed in front of the church entry but sometimes behind the chevet.

Baldachin: a structure that symbolically protects the high altar or the baptismal font, composed of a covering usually supported by four small columns with capitals, connected by arches or architraves.

Baptistery: from the Latin *baptisterium,* bath or pool. The place where early Christians performed the rite of purification by water, or the sacrament of baptism. Starting in the fourth century, it became an independent edifice conceived especially for the administration of baptism, with a central plan, either square, circular, or polygonal in shape, located adjacent to or near the church.

Base: the lowest element of a vertical support, generally composed of a carved element on a square or polygonal (uncarved) the plinth.

Basilica: from the Greek *basilikä,* royal porch, then from the Latin *basilica.* In the Roman Empire, a rectangular edifice divided into a nave and aisles separated by rows of columns or pillars, terminating in one of its ends by an apse, the whole covered by a timber roof. It served as a court of justice and a meeting hall. The Christian basilica presented the same basic plan, with a central nave higher than the aisles. It was entered through one of the short sides, and the opposite end terminated in one or more apses, the main one having a width similar to that of the central have of the edifice.

Beatus: commentary on the Apocalypse written by the Abbot Beatus of the monastery of Liébana in Asturias at the end of the eighth century.

Canon: clergyman who follows the canons of the Church. Beginning in the Carolingian period, canons lived together in a religious community, near a collegiate church or a cathedral, and followed their own rule.

Capital: from the Latin *caput,* head. Architectural element surmounting a column or other vertical support that receives the load from an architrave or arch.

Catacombs: ensemble of a complex of subterranean galleries used as a cemetery, which sometimes was enlarged by the use of chambers called *cubicula.*

Catechumen: individual receiving religious instruction with the goal of baptism.

Cathedral: from the Latin *cathedra,* chair, bishop's throne. Principal church of a diocese and the primary place of worship in the episcopal see. Beginning in the Carolingian period, it was run by a chapter of canons.

Cella: the space in a non-Christian temple reserved for the priests; it housed the image of the deity.

Chancel: from the Latin *cancellus,* railing. Railing or low enclosure usually composed of sculpted slabs and stone or marble pillars. Separates the space reserved for the clergy from the nave, where the congregation sits.

Chapter: canonical or monastic assembly at which a chapter of the Rule was read to begin the assembly. A college of canons ran the collegiate church of a cathedral.

Chevron: geometric decorative motif in the shape of a zigzag.

Choir: from the Latin *chorus.* Liturgical section of a church reserved for the singers and clergy, often placed at the east in a church facing east. The choir generally gives onto the chevet and sometimes onto a section of the nave. By extension, the word is applied to the western space reserved for singers.

Ciborium: in Antiquity, a baldachin used to shelter the statue of the divinity. In Christian architecture, a light construction carried on slender columns and connected by architraves or arches that symbolically protects the high altar or the baptismal font.

Cloister: from the Latin *claustrum, claudere,* to close. Court or courtyard, often square or rectangular, bordered by an open colonnade, reserved for monks or nuns and surrounded by the major edifices of the monastic life.

Codex: manuscript book composed of folded and sewn pages, assembled into stitched sections.

Coffer: hollow panel in a ceiling or in an arch soffit.

Collegiate church: a church, generally surrounded by monastic buildings, run by a chapter of canons.

Colophon: text that concludes a manuscript and that often provides information on its commission or execution.

Column: vertical architectural support composed of a shaft supported on a base and crowned by a capital.

Confessio: from the Latin *confessio,* public declaration. The place where the body of a martyr (or, later, of a confessor) was deposed. By extension, the sepulchral vault under the sanctuary of a church that contains the tomb of a saint.

Consecration: rite that sanctifies a place of worship by dedicating it to God. In the paleo-Christian period, it consisted essentially of the deposition of relics under the altar.

Council: from the Latin *concilium.* Assembly of bishops who establish texts and canons and issue decrees on problems of doctrine and ecclesiastical discipline.

Counter-apse: western apse

Crypt: from the Latin *crypta,* subterranean gallery, sepulchral vault. Vaulted space most often placed under a church, usually under the choir, that generally used to hold tombs.

Cupola: hemispherical vault that usually covers a square surface.

Diocese: from the Greek, then the Latin *dioecesis.* Beginning in the fourth century, an administrative district grouping together several parishes; later, an ecclesiastical district under the control of the bishop, which often corresponded to the old city area.

Diptych: from the Greek, then the Latin *diptychum*. Tablet in wood, ivory, or precious metal with two wings capable of folding together, fastened by hinges, and whose interior faces were covered with a fine layer of wax. The names of the living and the dead for whom services were held were inscribed on the liturgical diptych.

Dome: a roof in the form of a sphere that rose over certain parts of the church. Often synonymous with *cupola*.

Entablature: horizontal crowning of an architectural order comprising a cornice, a frieze, and an architrave.

Extrados: upper, outer curved face of a vault or an arch or, sometimes, of a lintel course or lintel.

Fenestella: small opening made in the vault or in a wall of the *confessio* that permitted the faithful to see and sometimes touch the sepulcher of a martyr or saint.

Hypogeum: underground room, generally funerary, hollowed out or constructed.

Hypostyle: room whose ceiling is supported by columns.

Interlace: decorative motif created from intertwined lines imitating braids and basketwork.

Intrados: lower, inner face of a vault or arch, also called a soffit.

Keystone: from the Latin *clavis*, key. Stone in the form of a wedge in a lintel, vault, or arch.

Lintel: horizontal member in wood or stone that closes the upper part of an opening and that supports the masonry.

Martyrium: construction rising over the site of the martyrdom or tomb of a martyr. By extension, a commemorative funerary edifice, generally square, polygonal, or semicircular in plan.

Mausoleum: from the name of King Mausolus of Halicarnassus in Asia Minor, who built a spectacular tomb for himself. Funerary monument intended to hold one or more sepulchers,

usually circular or polygonal in shape. In paleo-Christian architecture, a monumental tomb.

Memoria: mention of the deceased, the relics of a martyr, or the funerary structure built in the martyr's memory.

Monastery: from the Latin *monasterium*. Group of buildings intended to accommodate a community of monks or nuns.

Narthex: in Early Christian architecture, the gallery, vestibule, or porch located in front of the main entrance of a church. Catechumens and those not baptized were not, at one stage, allowed to enter the church, and followed the liturgical ceremonies from this spot. It often streched the entire width of the main façade.

Nave: in a rectangular church, the central space between the front façade and the entrance to the apse or the crossing.

Paradise: closed or open space found in front of some churches; also known as a parvis.

Pendentive: small supporting vault through which a change in plan can be effected on any level of the construction.

Peristyle: originally, a gallery with columns or colonnade that surrounded a court in domestic Roman architecture. By extension, a court surrounded by galleries in domestic, palatine, or public architecture in Antiquity.

Pilaster: rectangular or shallow vertical support placed against a wall or let into the wall, sometimes having a base and a capital.

Pillar: rectangular or polygonal vertical support.

Plan: representation of a construction showing a horizontal section on the floor level.

Podium: raised base reached by a few steps.

Portico: from the Latin *porticus*. Gallery that opens onto the outdoors located on the ground floor or the first floor and supported by columns. In the Middle Ages, this term replaced *narthex*.

Presbytery: the part of the church reserved for the bishop and priests; in the West, it is generally located in or in front of the apse.

Relics: the bodily remains of a saint or clothing and objects associated with him or her.

Reliquary: chest holding the relics of a saint that can be displayed to the faithful.

Rotunda: circular-plan edifice, usually covered with a timber roof or a dome.

Saddleback roof: two opposing pitched faces joined at the top.

Sanctuary: section of a church reserved for the clergy that contains the altar and where the liturgy is performed.

Stylobate: masonry base on which a colonnade or order of pilasters rests.

Synod: meeting of the priests and bishops of a province, convened by the archbishop.

Titulus: in paleo-Christian Rome, a church designated by the name of its owner and that made frequent use of clergy.

Tower: building or building element, square, circular, or polygonal, distinguished by its dimension of height.

Transept: transverse part of a church that intersects the longitudinal body of the edifice at a right angle and separates the chevet from the nave. The "crossing" is the intersection of the main space of the edifice and the transept. The arms are the two parts of the transept that extend from either side of the crossing; these are often of the same width as the nave and aisles.

Translation of relics: liturgical displacement of relics from one place to another. This transfer often accompanies the dedication of a church.

Triclinium: dining room in an ancient Roman house/palace.

Vault: masonry structure that covers a space between two lateral walls and that presents an intrados and an extrados. The *barrel vault* has a semicircular form that resembles a

half cylinder; the *rib vault* has a framework of diagonal arched ribs the *cul-de-four vault* is a half cupola that customarily covers the apses; the *groin vault* is formed by the right-angled intersection of two barrel vaults.

Villa: rural group, often agricultural, comprising the owner's dwelling and various attached structures, and sometimes a chapel. In particular, the residence in such a complex.

Voussoir: wedge-shaped stones in arches and vaults on both the intrados and extrados.

Westwork: from the German *westwerk*. Group of architectural structures placed opposite the choir of a church, generally at the entrance, which may include one or more towers, a porch, a high gallery, the first bays of the nave, and sometimes a counter-choir.

BIBLIOGRAPHY

Atti dell'ottavo congresso di studi sull'alto medioevo, Milan, 1962.

Barral i Altet, X.: *L'art pre-romànic a Catalunya,* Segles IX–X, Barcelona, 1981.

Barral i Altet, X. (ed.): *Artistes, artisans et production artistique au Moyen Age,* 3 vols., Paris, 1986–1990.

Barral i Altet, X.: *L'art médiéval,* (Que sais-je?), Paris, 1991.

Beckwith, J.: *Early Medieval Art. Carolingian, Ottonian, Romanesque,* London, 1977.

Bianchi Bandinelli, R.: *Dall'elenismo al medioevo,* Rome, 1978.

Bognetti, G. P., G. Chierici, and A. de Capitani d'Arzago: *Santa Maria di Castelseprio,* Milan, 1948.

Bonet Correa, A.: *Arte pre-románico asturiano,* Barcelona, 1967.

Braunfels, W. et alii: *Karl der Große,* 5 vols., Düsseldorf, 1965–1967.

Braunfels, W.: *Die Welt der Karolinger und ihre Kunst,* Munich, 1968.

Brenk, B.: *Tradition und Neuerung in der christlichen Kunst des ersten Jahrtausends,* Munich, 1924.

Bruce-Mitford, R.: *The Sutton Hoo Ship-Burial,* 3 vols., London, 1975–1984.

Bullough, D. A.: *The Age of Charlemagne,* London, 1965.

Campbell, J., E. John, and P. Vormald: *The Anglo-Saxons,* Oxford, 1982.

La cattedra lignea di S. Pietro in Vaticano, Atti della pontifica Accademia romana di archeologia, Memorie, Rome, 1971.

Cechelli, C.: *I monumenti del Friuli dal secolo IV all'XI. I. Cividale,* Milan, 1943.

Charlemagne, œuvre, rayonnement et survivances, exhibition catalogue, Aachen, 1965.

La civiltà dei Longobardi in Europa, Atti del Convegno dell'Accademia nazionale dei lincei (Roma–Cividale del Friuli, 1971), Rome, 1974.

Conant, K. J.: *Carolingian and Romanesque Architecture 800–1200,* (The Pelican History of Art), Harmondsworth, 1966, reprint New Haven–London, 1993.

Congrès international pour l'étude de l'art du Haut Moyen Age, 10 vols., 1949–1962.

Corboz, A.: *Le Haut Moyen Age,* Fribourg, 1970.

Corzo Sánchez, R.: *San Pedro de la Nave,* Zamora, 1986.

La cultura in Italia fra tardo Antico e alto Medioevo, Atti del Convegno tenuto a Roma, Consiglio nazionale delle ricerche, 1979, 2 vols., Rome, 1981.

Doppelfeld, O., and W. Weyers: *Die Ausgrabungen im Dom zum Köln,* Mainz, 1980.

Durliat, M.: *L'architecture espagnole,* Paris, 1966.

Durliat, M.: *Des barbares à l'an Mil,* Paris, 1985.

Effmann, W.: *Centula Saint-Riquier. Eine Untersuchung zur Geschichte der kirchlichen Baukunst in der Karolingerzeit,* Münster, 1912.

Effmann, W.: *Die Kirche der Abtei Corvey,* ed. posth. by A. Fuchs, Paderborn, 1929.

Elbern, V. H.: *Das Erste Jahrtausend,* 3 vols., Düsseldorf, 1962–1964.

Études mérovingiennes. Actes des journées de Poitiers, 1952, Poitiers, 1953.

Ewig, E.: *Spätantikes und fränkisches Gallien,* 2 vols., Munich, 1976–1979.

Fernie, E.: *The Architecture of the Anglo-Saxons,* London, 1983.

Fillitz, H.: *Das Mittelalter,* I, Propyläen Kunstgeschichte, Berlin, 1969.

Fisher, E. A.: *An Introduction to Anglo-Saxon Architecture and Sculpture,* London, 1959.

Fontaine, J.: *Isidore de Séville et la culture classique dans l'Espagne wisigothique,* Etudes augustiniennes, 3 vols., Paris, 1959.

Fontaine, J.: *L'art pré-roman hispanique,* vol. I, 1973; *L'art mozarabe,* vol. II, 1977.

Fossier, R. et alii: *Le Moyen Age,* I, Les Mondes nouveaux, 390–950, Paris, 1982.

Fossier, R. (ed.): *The Cambridge Illustrated History of the Middle Ages,* vol. 1, 350–950, Cambridge, 1986.

Fournier, G.: *Les Mérovingiens,* Paris, 1966.

Gibson, M., J. Nelson (eds.), and D. Ganz: *Charles the Bald: Court and Kingdom,* London, 1981.

Gómez Moreno, M.: *Iglesias mozárabes, Arte español de los siglos IX a XI,* Granada, 1975.

Grabar, A.: *Martyrium,* Paris, 1946.

Grabar, A.: *L'art de la fin de l'Antiquité et du Moyen Age,* 3 vols., Paris, 1968.

Grabar, A.: *Les voies de la création en iconographie chrétienne. Antiquité et Moyen Age,* Paris, 1979.

Grabar, A., and C. Nordenfalk: *Early Medieval Painting from the Fourth to the Eleventh Century,* New York, 1957.

Haseloff, A.: *Pre-Romanesque Sculpture in Italy,* New York, 1971.

Heitz, C.: *L'Architecture religieuse carolingienne. Les formes et leurs fonctions,* Paris, 1980.

Heitz, C.: *Gallia praeromanica. Die Kunst der merowingischen, karolingischen und frühromanischen Epoche in Frankreich,* Vienna, 1982.

Henderson, G.: *Early Medieval* (Style and Civilisation), Harmondsworth, 1977, reprint, Toronto, 1993.

Henry, F.: *L'Art irlandais,* 3 vols., Paris, 1963–1964.

Horn, W., and E. Born: *The Plan of St. Gall,* 3 vols., Berkeley, Los Angeles, London, 1979.

Hubert, J.: *L'Art pré-roman,* Paris, 1938.

Hubert, J.: *L'Architecture religieuse du Haut Moyen Age en France,* Paris, 1952.

Hubert, J.: *Arts et vie sociale de la fin du monde antique au Moyen Age,* Geneva, 1977.

Hubert, J.: *Nouveau Recueil d'études d'archéologie et d'histoire de la fin du monde antique au Moyen Age,* Geneva, 1985.

Hubert, J., J. Porcher, and W. F. Volbach: *Europe of the Invasions,* New York, 1969.

Hubert, J., J. Porcher, and W. F. Volbach: *The Carolingian Renaissance,* New York, 1970.

Intellectuels et artistes dans l'Europe carolingienne IX–XIe siècles, exhibition catalogue, Auxerre, 1990.

Junyent, E.: *L'Arquitectura religiosa a Catalunya abans del Romànic,* Montserrat, 1983.

Kendrick, T. D.: *Anglo-Saxon Art to A.D. 900,* London, 1938.

Kitzinger, E.: *The Art of Byzantium and the Medieval West. Selected Studies,* Bloomington, 1976.

Koch, G.: *Early Christian Art and Architecture,* London, 1996.

Krautheimer, R.: *Studies in Early Christian, Medieval and Renaissance Art,* New York, 1969.

Krautheimer, R.: *Early Christian and Byzantine Architecture,* (Pelican History of Art), Harmondsworth, 1965; 4th rev. ed., New Haven, 1986.

Kreusch, F.: *Beobachtungen an der Westanlage der Klosterkirche zu Corvey,* Cologne, Graz, 1963.

Kubach, H. E. and V. H. Elbern: *Das frühmittelalterliche Imperium,* Baden-Baden, 1968.

Kubach, H. E., and A. Verbeek: *Romanische Baukunst an Rhein und Maas. Katalog der vorromanischen und romanischen Denkmäler,* Berlin, 1976.

Lasko, P.: *Ars Sacra 800–1200,* The Pelican History of Art, Harmondsworth-Baltimore, 1972.

Le Goff, J.: *Medieval Civilization 400–1500,* Oxford and New York, 1988.

Lehmann, E.: *Der frühe deutsche Kirchenbau. Die Entwicklung seiner Raumordnung bis 1080,* Berlin, 1938.

Longobardi e Lombardia: aspetti di civiltà longobarda, Atti del 6° Congresso internazionale di stui sull'alto Medioevo, 1978, 2 vols., Spoleto, 1980.

Lopez, R. S.: *Naissance de l'Europe,* Paris, 1962.

L'Orange, H. P., and H. Torp: *Il "Tempietto" longobardo di Cividale,* 3 vols., Rome, 1977–1979.

Louis, R.: *Autessiodorum Christianum. Les églises d'Auxerre, des origines au XIe siècle,* Paris, 1952.

Maillé, Marquise de: *Les cryptes de Jouarre,* Paris, 1971.

Mauer, H. et alii: *Die Abtei Reichenau,* Sigmaringen, 1974.

Messerer, W.: *Karolingische Kunst,* Cologne, 1973.

Musset, L.: *Les peuples scandinaves au Moyen Age,* Paris, 1951.

Musset, L.: *Les invasions,* 2 vols., Paris, 1965.

Naissance des arts chrétiens. Atlas des monuments paléochrétiens de la France, Paris, 1991.

Nuñez, M.: *Historia de arquitectura galega. Arquitectura preromanica,* Santiago, 1978.

Nuove ricerche sulla cattedra lignea di San Pietro in Vaticano, Atti della pontifica Accademia romana di archeologia, Memorie, Rome, 1975.

Oakeshott, W.: *Classical Inspiration in Medieval Art,* London, 1959.

Onofrio, M. d': *Roma e Aquisgrana,* Rome, 1983.

Oswald, F., L. Schaeffer, and H. R. Sennhauser: *Vorromanische Kirchenbauten. Katalog der Denkmäler bis zum Ausgang der Ottonen,* 3 vols., Munich, 1966–1971.

Palol Salellas, P. de: *Early Medieval Art in Spain,* London, 1967.

Palol Salellas, P. de: *Arqueología cristiana de la España romana,* siglos IV–VI, Madrid, Valladolid, 1967.

Palol Salellas, P. de: *Hispanic Art of the Visigothic Period,* New York, 1968.

Pita Andrade, J. M.: *Arte asturiano,* Madrid, 1963.

Les premiers monuments chrétiens de la France, Paris, 1965.

Premiers temps chrétiens en Gaule méridionale, exhibition catalogue, Lyons, 1986.

Price, L.: *The Plan of St. Gall in Brief,* Berkeley, Los Angeles, London, 1982.

Puertas Tricas, R.: *Iglesias hispánicas,* siglos IV al VIII, Madrid, 1975.

Puig i Cadafalch, J.: *Le premier art roman,* Paris, 1928.

Puig i Cadafalch, J.: *La géographie et les origines du premier art roman,* Paris, 1930.

Puig i Cadafalch, J.: *L'art wisigothique et ses survivances,* Paris, 1961.

Rasmo, N.: *Arte carolingia in Alto Adige,* Bolzano, 1981.

Recueil général des monuments sculptés en France pendant le Haut Moyen Age (IVᵉ–Xᵉ siècle), Paris, 1978 ff.

Riché, P.: *Education and Culture in the Barbarian West, Sixth through Eighth Centuries,* Columbia, S.C., 1976.

Roma e l'età carolingia, Atti delle giornate di studio 3–8 maggio 1976, Università di Roma, Rome, 1976.

Romanelli, P., and P. J. Nothagen: *S. Maria Antiqua,* Rome, 1964.

Rouche, M.: *L'Aquitaine des wisigoths aux Arabes 418–781,* Paris, 1979.

Schlosser, J. von: *Schriftquellen zur Geschichte der karolingischen Kunst,* Vienna, 1892.

Schlunk, H., and T. Hauschild: *Hispania Antiqua. Die Denkmäler der frühchristlichen und westgotischen Zeit,* Mainz, 1978.

Schmid, A. A. et alii: *Riforma religiosa e arti nell'epoca carolingia,* Bologna, 1983.

Schnitzler, H.: *Die vorromanische Kunst,* Düsseldorf, 1957.

Schramm, P. E.: *Kaiser, Rom und Renovatio,* Leipzig, Berlin, 1929.

Schramm, P. E, and F. Mütherich: *Denkmale der deutschen Könige und Kaiser. Ein Beitrag zur Herrschergeschichte von Karl dem Großen bis Friedrich II. 768–1250,* Munich, 1962.

Settimane di studio del Centro italiano di studi sull'alto medioevo, Spoleto.

Shetelig, H.: *Classical Impulses in Scandinavian Art from the Migration Period to the Viking Age,* Oslo, 1949.

Symposium sobre cultura asturiana de la alta edad media, 1961, Oviedo, 1967.

Synthronon. Art et archéologie de la fin de l'Antiquité et du Moyen Age, Paris, 1968.

Talbot Rice, D.: *English Art, 871–1100,* Oxford, 1952.

Tardo Antico e Alto Medioevo. La forma artistica dal passagio nel Antichità al Medioevo, Atti del Convegno internazionale della Accademia nazionale dei lincei, 1967, Rome, 1968.

Taylor, H. M. T., and J. Taylor: *Anglo-Saxon Architecture,* 3 vols., Cambridge, 1965–1978.

Verbeek, A.: *Kölner Kirchen. Die kirchliche Baukunst in Köln von den Anfängen bis zur Gegenwart,* Cologne, 1959.

Verzone, P.: *L'Arte preromanica en Liguria ed i relievi decorativi dei "secoli barbari",* Turin, 1945.

Verzone, P.: *The Art of Europe: The Dark Ages from Theodoric to Charlemagne,* New York, 1968.

Un village au temps de Charlemagne. Moines et paysans de l'abbaye de Saint-Denis du VIIᵉ siècle à l'an Mil, exhibition catalogue, Paris, 1988.

Villalón, M. C.: *Mérida visigoda,* Badajoz, 1985.

Volbach, W. F.: *The Carolingian Renaissance,* New York, 1970.

Webster, L., and J. Backhouse (eds.): *The Making of England. Anglo-Saxon Art and Culture AD 600–900,* exhibition catalogue, London, 1991.

Weitzmann, K.: *Age of Spirituality. Late Antique and Early Christian Art Third to Seventh Century,* exhibition catalogue, New York, 1979.

Weitzmann, K. (ed.): *A Symposium,* New York, 1980.

Weitzmann, K.: *Art in the Medieval West and Its Contacts with Byzantium,* London, 1982.

Werdendes Abendland an Rhein und Ruhr, exhibition catalogue, Essen, 1956.

Werner, K. F.: *Histoire de France. Les origines (avant l'An Mil),* Paris, 1984.

Werner, K. F.: *Vom Frankenreich zur Entfaltung Deutschlands und Frankreichs,* Sigmaringen, 1984.

Wilson, D. M. (ed.) et alii: *The Northern World: The History and Heritage of Northern Europe, AD 400–1100,* New York, 1980.

Wilson, D. M.: *Anglo-Saxon Art from the Seventh Century to the Norman Conquest,* 1984.

Wormald, F.: *Collected Writings I: Studies in Medieval Art from the Sixth to the Twelfth Centuries,* Oxford, 1984.

Yarza, J.: *Arte y arquitectura en España, 500–1250,* Madrid, 1979.

Index – Monuments

Index– Persons

ACKNOWLEDGEMENTS AND CREDITS

The majority of the photographs illustrating this book have been taken by Claude Huber, Lausanne, and by Anne and Henri Stierlin, Geneva. The photographs of the latter are found on pages 3, 10–11, 13, 16–21, 24–26, 34, 42, 60–61, 63–65, 71, 84–85, 97–117, 125, 161–165, 172–173, 183–184, 192–221, 224–225.

The author, the photographers, and the publisher wish to express their sincere appreciation to the authorities of the various countries concerned for granting permission to photograph the historic monuments illustrated in this book. They owe a special debt of gratitude to the directors of the museums, libraries, and treasuries who gave them access to objects and manuscripts in their collections. This pertains to the following:

Trésor de L'Abbaye de Saint-Maurice d'Agaune,
Musée d'Art et d'Histoire, Geneva,
Musée Cantonal de Lausanne,
Trésor de l'Abbaye de Sainte-Foy, Conques,
Musée National du Bardo, Tunis,
Museo Arqueológico, Madrid,
Biblioteca Nacional, Madrid,
Biblioteca del monastero real del El Escorial ,
Museo diocesano, Girona,
Tesoro de la Cámara Santa, Oviedo,
Abadía de Santo Domingo de Silos.

In addition, they gratefully acknowledge the documentation helpfully provided by various institutions and photographers, in particular:

Pages 5, 123, 126, 140, 153: © Library of the abbey of St. Gall.
Page 62: © Charles Bonnet, Geneva.
Page 135: © Giraudon, Paris.
Pages 14, 32, 33: © Ursula Held, Ecublens.
Page 222: © Lauros-Giraudon, Paris.
Pages 58, 59: © Monde de la Bible 1996/Jean-Benoît Héron.
Pages 186, 187: © Werner Neumeister, Munich.
Page 29: © SCALA, Antella (Florence).
Page 22 above: © Josef Tietzen, Trier.
Page 22 below: © Yaph, Trier.

Finally, the plans illustrated on pages 8, 9, 17, 20, 27, 28, 35, 44, 49, 56, 60, 64, 80, 84, 87, 90, 101, 104, 114, 122, 128, 134, 135, 140, 146, 150, 152, 158, 159, 171, 174, 179, 181, 189, 193, 194, 200, 201, 206, 209, 214, 216, 218, and 224 were created especially for this book by Alberto Berengo Gardin, Milan.

The author would like to thank Alix de Bellegarde and Sophie Le Pennec for their help with documentation.

All 40 titles at a glance

Each book: US$ 29.99 | £ 16.99 | CDN$ 39.95

The Ancient World
▶ The Near East
▶ Egypt
▶ Greece
▶ The Roman Empire
▶ The Greco-Roman Orient

The Medieval World
▶ Byzantium
▶ The Early Middle Ages
▶ The Romanesque
▶ High Gothic
▶ Late Gothic

The Pre-Colombian World
▶ The Maya
▶ Mexico
▶ The Aztecs
▶ Peru
▶ The Incas

Islamic Masterpieces
▶ Islam from Baghdad to Cordoba
▶ Islam from Cairo to Granada
▶ Persia
▶ Asia Minor
▶ Mughal

The Splendours of Asia
▶ Hindu India
▶ Buddhist India
▶ China
▶ South-East Asia
▶ Japan

Stylistic Developments from 1400
▶ Renaissance
▶ Baroque in Italy
▶ Baroque in Central Europe
▶ Hispanic Baroque
▶ French Classicism

The Modern Age
▶ Neo-Classicism and Revolution
▶ American Architecture
▶ Art nouveau
▶ Early Modern Architecture
▶ Visionary Masters
▶ International Style
▶ Post-Modernism
▶ Green Architecture
▶ New Forms
▶ Contemporary Masters

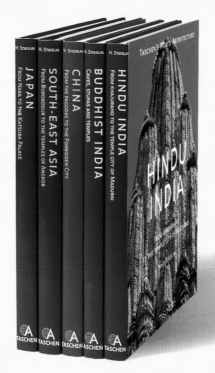

"... a truly remarkable publishing event in architecture"
The Architectural Review
London

▶ Collect 40 volumes of TASCHEN'S WORLD ARCHITECTURE in eight years (1996–2003) and build up a complete panorama of world architecture from the earliest buildings of Mesopotamia to the latest contemporary projects.

▶ The series is grouped into five-volume units, each devoted to the architectural development of a major civilisation, and introducing the reader to many new and unfamiliar worlds.

▶ Each volume covers a complex architectural era and is written so vividly that most readers will feel the urge to go out and discover these magnificent buildings for themselves.

TASCHEN'S WORLD ARCHITECTURE

▶ TASCHEN'S WORLD ARCHITECTURE presents 6000 years of architectural history in 40 volumes.

▶ Each volume is a detailed and author-itative study of one specific era.

▶ The whole series provides a compre-hensive survey of architecture from antiquity to the present day. Five volumes will be published each year.

▶ TASCHEN'S WORLD ARCHITECTURE is a must for all lovers of architecture and travel.

▶ Renowned photographers have travelled the world for this series, presenting more than 12000 photographs of famous and lesser-known buildings.

▶ Expert authors guide the reader through TASCHEN'S WORLD ARCHI-TECTURE with exciting, scientifically well-founded texts that place architec-ture within the cultural, political and social context of each era.

▶ The elegant, modern design and the clear, visually striking layout guide the reader through the historical and contemporary world of architecture.

▶ Influential architectural theories, typical stylistic features and specific construction techniques are separately explained on eye-catching pages.

▶ Each volume includes between 40 and 50 maps, plans and structural drawings based on the latest scholarly findings and are produced for this series using state-of-the-art computer technology.

▶ The appendix contains clear chronolo-gical tables, giving an instant overview of the correlation between the histor-ical events and architecture of any given civilisation.

▶ A detailed glossary clearly explains architectural terms.

▶ An index of names and places ensures quick and easy reference to specific buildings and people.

▶ Each book contains 240 pages with some 300 color illustrations on high-quality art paper. 240 x 300 mm, hardcover with dust jacket.

Each book: US$ 29.99 | £ 16.99 | CDN$ 39.95